"STARbooks continues to put out the big ones! John Patrick does it again in 'The Best of the Superstars ...'
Here the reader will discover 'brusque vignettes' about our favorite malerotic stars and other luscious boy-boys. Yum!"
-Jesse Monteagudo,
The Weekly News, Miami.

THE BEST OF THE SUPERSTARS 1992: THE YEAR IN SEX

Edited by John Patrick

One of a series from STARbooks Press
Sarasota, FL

Books by John Patrick
Non-Fiction
The Best of the Superstars
A Charmed Life: Vince Cobretti
Lowe Down: Tim Lowe
The Best of the Superstars 1991
Legends: The World's Sexiest Men, Vol. 1
The Best of the Superstars 1992
Fiction
Billy & David: A Deadly Minuet
The Bigger They Are...
The Younger They Are...
The Harder They Are...
Angel: The Complete Trilogy
Angel II: Stacy's Story
Angel: The Complete Quintet
A Natural Beauty (Ed.)
The Kid (with Joe Leslie)
STRIP: He Danced Alone
Huge (Ed.)

Library of Congress ISSN No. 1053-6671
ISBN No. 1-877978-28-0

Contents of The Best of the Superstars 1992
The Year in Sex

Introduction: Public Sex & Pee-wee

Introduction

Public Sex and Pee-wee

"What two people were shot in the back of the head in a theater?"

"Abraham Lincoln and the man who was sitting in front of Pee-wee Herman."

The infamous Pee-wee Herman affair set the tone for the year in sex, a year when celebrities bristled more than ever at the thought they might be linked with queers or, horror of horrors, be labeled one.

"Going public," in more ways than one, has long obsessed many gay males: "Many gay men desire privileged categories of people and masculine ideals drawn from the dominant heterosexual culture," Thomas Almaguer, who teaches sociology at the University of California at Berkeley, says. "The most respectable of these is the upper-class, waspy Ralph Lauren or Calvin Klein man. Others eschew these well-heeled social categories and desire more rugged, working class heterosexual men from various racial and ethnic backgrounds. These sexual desires often lead men into sites where this particular masculinity is affirmed and valorized: gymnasiums, public parks, locker rooms, bars and also truck stops, bus depots, public squares, adult bookstores, public restrooms and certain streets. These are male domains where straight working-class men frequently congregate and affirm their manhood; they often are hot houses of raw masculinity."

Such a "hot house" is the old-fashioned XXX-rated theater south of downtown Sarasota, Florida, the only such venue in the County. It was here, in his hometown for chrissakes, the actor Paul Reubens, who had made a small fortune being something other than himself, namely Pee-wee Herman, fell from grace. Being a citizen of the fair county where all the action took place, I took special interest in the case. I discovered that the reason police patrol the theater is to, in the words of an undercover cop, "keep it safe" for the straights:

"They don't like to be bothered by gay men." News to me.

As Almaguer states: "These are precisely the places where gay men seek the 'kindness of strangers' that straight men offer. These impersonal sexual encounters are usually cloaked in silence, no one need say a word. To do so would risk exploding the erotic fantasy that guides gay male ventures into such scenes. These ritualized and scripted encounters would be meaningless if these strangers turned out to be 'girls.' Each person's sexual identity is not compromised as long as they do not violate the gendered role they play (like the ostensibly straight man allowing himself to be penetrated)."

In the dark confines of the theater, it was well-reported, Pee-wee twice exposed himself and masturbated in front of an undercover policeman. Columnist David Olinger wrote: "Poor Pee-wee. He was our weirdo of the week. I gabbed about him. Everybody I know did. How could we help it? The story was too good to ignore. (Pee-wee) stepped out of character. All of a sudden he's a real guy with a booking photo. A guy with a goatee who doesn't look like Pee-wee. A guy who looks to our adult eyes like somebody with a sexual problem. This we can't forgive."

This "problem," as Olinger characterizes it, is one that exists because there is little institutional support for homosexuality in this society. "It is not surprising," Almague asserts, "that gay male relationships and sexual conduct are incessantly driven underground. Even the most open of gay men are forced to conceal aspects of their otherwise respectable relationships and sexual practices from some people. The symbol for the closet captures this reality very well. As a result, it is inevitable that many gay men go looking for love in all the wrong places. Why? Because there is little social space outside of gay ghettos for gay relationships to flourish. Moreover, most men- gay or straight - simply have not developed the emotional capacity to enter into meaningful and satisfying relationships in the first place."

A reporter for the *National Enquirer* commented: "When you come up with something that is totally unbelievable but true, people go, 'My God!' There's a shock value to it. It allows them to feel superior saying, 'Well, I knew that all along. I saw Pee-wee prancing around.'"

Granted, impersonal, public expression of sexuality, of "prancing around," provides an implicit challenge to the dominant order. But, in this most crime-ridden of nations, is it worth six hours a day of three cops' precious time? Wouldn't the time be better spent corraling drug pushers? That's what the newspapers, most of the thoughtful citizenry of Sarasota, and people all over the country were asking as well, putting "victimless crimes" in sharper focus.

Public Defender Elliot Metcalfe said, "There are serious crimes being committed and we have deputies sitting around a dirty movie house. While Sheriff Monge said there was no outpouring of complaints about the theater, on occasions when an undercover drug deal falls through, 'You have a squad of folks sitting around with nothing to do. Instead of having them sit around for the rest of the evening, they go to adult theaters.' Can't you just picture the scene? 'Hey, guys, I'm bored as shit, let's go bust some weirdos.' 'Ya man, we haven't gotten our rocks off in weeks.'" Or, as Tom Teepen in the *Atlanta Constitution* put it, "Is that a great job or what? Imagine coming home at night after work: 'Hi, honey, I'm home.' 'Hello, dear. How was your day?' Now, how in the hell do you answer that one?"

Truth be known, the survelliance of the theater is a constant part of the routine of the sheriff's department. My sources told me that the deputies, numbering from three to six guys, are in the theater twice a month, for five to six hours at a stretch, sometimes sitting in the theater while it is completely empty, waiting for up to an hour for people to show up. On that hot night in July, the sheriff's "porno patrol" numbered four, dressed in T-shirts and cut-off jeans. The manager commented that he'd always been annoyed at how scruffy the deputies looked; they certainly stood out from the crowd, who he says have a "country club" look. The cops had arrived around five and stayed 5 1/2 hours. In that time, they arrested four men. The ticket seller is forbidden from mentioning there are cops in the house; to do so would make him subject to arrest himself for obstruction of justice. The man known about town as Mr. Chatterbox, and an intimate of the Reubens family for many years, described the scene: "After Paul paid the $8 admission, he entered the theater, a rather grand space that appears larger than its 120-seat capacity. Red sound curtains line the walls and there is a strong smell of disinfectant. Six ceiling fans kick up a breeze; combined with the air conditioning, which comes on with a roar that makes everybody flinch, it could easily have been the coolest place in town. The theater was not full. Although it was Friday, the day after the features change, if 20 people are there at any given time, it's a crowd. Paul chose a seat in the third row from the rear, toward the end farthest from the entrance. According to deputies, he masturbated twice, once at 8:25 and then again 10 minutes later. The police report gets quite specific. It is this attention to detail, perhaps, that makes you feel when you read it that someone is being spied on in a private act. How long Paul remained in the theater after being observed is unclear: One report says five minutes, another says an hour. At any rate, as he was leaving, he was told by deputies he was under arrest and led to the parking lot."

Paul said he knew that people got in trouble trying to fool around with other people in the theater but he thought it was all right if he was by himself. Then he tried to avoid the arrest by offering to perform a benefit. The deputies would have none of it; they took him in, booked him and charged him with Exposure of Sexual Organs.

When the public outcry began, the Sheriff circled the wagons around the department and refused to consider constructive criticism. The city's key media, the *Herald Tribune*, owned by *The New York Times*, editorialized: "...The vice squad has enormous latitude. That's a dangerous practice, both for the public and the deputies themselves. Sheriff Monge has a duty to his department and the public to roll with the punches and reassess the priorities of his department. Undoubtedly he could find better ways to deploy his deputies."

These were the same deputies who, a few weeks before, had arrested bathers at the gay end of the beach for wearing outrageous T-back bathing suits and, in a prostitution sting, allowed two girls to fellate them and then have sex with each other before arresting them.

As Olinger said, "Mirror, mirror on the wall, who's the weirdest of us all?" When the Pee-wee incident broke in the national media, the Chamber of Commerce got dozens of calls from people saying they were never coming back to Sarasota, long thought to be nothing more than God's waiting room, a place wags had called "Shrivel City" and "Blue Hairs by the Bay." But if one offends the sensibilities of Middle America, locked in a vicious tabloid mentality, you can become a *cause celebre* in La Gran Manzana, which is often, as in this case, positively heartening. "We are all Pee-wee," said a poster plastered all around New York, juxtaposing Reubens' mug against the cherubic camp of his Pee-wee persona. "After all," asked the *Village Voice*, "how many of us survived adolescence without getting caught at least once with our pants down?" Pee-wee became a comic book renegade. It seemed as quickly as he was banned, he was embraced. Celebrant T-shirts were hot in L.A.: "Save Pee-wee!," "Keep Your Head Up, Pee-wee!," and "I'm Pulling for Pee-wee!."

Back in Manhattan, "Free Pee-wee!" sheet cakes, feeding 35, were selling for $100. At Toys-R-Us, all remaining Pee-wee toys were hot. "All of a sudden," a spokesman for the stores said, "people were asking for the doll. People are funny, aren't they?" And some 400 supporters of the comedian rallied in Greenwich Village to denounce his arrest. In the same week, Laurie Stone in the *Village Voice* commented: "Libido is always erupting out of him in the form of campy flounces, risque asides and hip wisecracks. He is resolutely deviant and accepting of other oddball types who light on planet Playhouse.

"Pee-wee impersonates the child deemed precocious by adults but who feels estranged within the world of other children. He's comfortable in fantasy, a realm where inanimate objects possess personality, sensibility, and where he is the ringmaster. His quirks, spaghetti limbs, a wobbly voice, an amorphous sexual identity - become a style esteemed and imitated by his fans. It's no wonder that children adore his freakishness: all kids feel dislocation amid grown-ups, steering through perilous, Brobdignagian landscapes, jealously beholding adult coordination, examining marked sexual difference, deciphering code-filled speech." And don't forget how close Pee-wee is to wee-wee. Of course, Pee-wee has always been a "wanker-figure, exulting in solitary, imaginative pleasure." The charges brought against Reubens have only made this association inescapable. Suddenly, solo sex had become a hot potato. Consider poor Joan Rivers, who thought the whole thing "terribly sad" and hoped Reubens would "go for help." To do what, find someone to jack him off?

Naturally, the true nature of Paul's sex life had become a matter of public concern. We knew that he lived alone in Studio City, California, but so do a lot of people. And we would occasionally hear about an indiscretion on Paul's part, such as being sighted at one of the city's gay bars on several occasions. These incidents could be passed off to the uninitiated because often such bars were trendy and attract the showbiz crowd. Mr. Chatterbox mentioned that he had a conversation with someone who claimed a sexual encounter with Paul. His report: "While I found the account convincing, what I remembered most are not the titillating details, they were in fact, rather banal, but the depressing resemblance the scene described had to the sex lives of so many unmarried, middle-aged men."

At the end of the sixth season of the "Playhouse," Paul said he'd like to kill off his character. The box he had built for himself was a formidable one indeed. Oddly enough, the scandal seems to have helped him escape. It made him grow up a bit, made him more appealing to an adult audience that had dismissed him. He's a talented, sensitive man who has provided enjoyment for a lot of people, not some hypocritical slimeball like Charles Keating who chiseled money from investors and the government while crusading against pornography. Reubens cared about the product he delivered to his audience and won awards for it. And, a few weeks after the brouhaha died down, the shrewd comic had the wisdom to appear on the MTV awards show, bringing down the house by asking, "Heard any good jokes lately?" *Rolling Stone* called it "a deafening and genuinely moving standing ovation." But California-based preacher James Dobson, Ph.D. (one of the original members of the Meese Commission) asked: "Is there a lesson here for young onlookers?"

A few weeks later, Reubens again publicly denied the charges, saying he was in the lobby at the time the officers claim they were watching him and he was in possession of the theater's own surveillance videotape, time-coded, to prove it. From police reports we were able to determine that, yes, Paul is left-handed, he's 5'-11" and weighs 135 pounds. The most interesting affidavit entries, though, regard the time of the crime ("2025 HRS") and the time of the arrest ("2150 HRS"). That means that 0125 HRS elapsed before the police nabbed the culprit. Thus, Paul's tape, if it exists, can discredit this testimony, but we'll never know because the star said he did not want to make the tape public to protect others in the theater at that time. Tape or no tape, his defense attorney Paul Rashkind thought the charge against his client should have been dismissed. He said: "Anyone going to an adult theater is expecting to see sexual organs. People don't go there for the popcorn." In the end, Pee-wee settled for a plea bargain, requiring him to plead no contest, do an anti-drug public service announcement, and perform 50 hours of community service. Larry Goldman, Reubens' publicist, said: "He's taking the plea to avoid the trial because of the stress that five days in court will put him through."

Another of his attorneys, Dan Dannheisser, said: "The only people who have a question about whether he's a good role model for kids are adults. I haven't seen any kids in that conversation. Given the need for role models, I think Paul Reubens is a great one." Remembering what Laurie Stone said, that Pee-wee has always been a "wanker-figure, exulting in solitary, imaginative pleasure," we couldn't agree with him more.

Another unintended public revelation occurred at the hands of the tabloid *Globe*, claiming to have an exclusive about singer/composer Neil Sedaka's penchant for muscular young men who "don't look gay." Marc Anthony, an escort service manager in Las Vegas, said that Sedaka was particularly turned on by blond hair and blue eyes and they had to be well endowed. Although he did his best to give the singer what he wanted, Anthony said Neil was a cheap trick. The going rate was $150 but Neil not only loves to make love to a callboy, he also loves to watch two of them get it on, so the rate should have been $300, but Neil would always haggle the price down to $250. And he never tipped the guys unless it was a dinner date. One hustler commented he only remembered one time when Neil got so carried away he actually joined them in bed, but stopped short of touching them. A hustler named Dex said the singer was "very warm and comfortable to be with. He would always ask what I wanted to do with my life and seemed genuinely interested. He'd give me advice. It was funny, one night I told him I wanted to be an actor and he warned me away from entering show business. He said that I should so something else because to succeed I might have to compromise my morals. I looked at him and said, 'What do you think I'm doing now?'" (Hell, kid, we just thought you were having fun.)

With homophobia reaching a fever pitch in Tinseltown, how should the press cover outing? The answer is, perhaps, don't bother. Ask Tom Selleck. The durable actor has lately become one of the most popular stars in America, in the most secret celebrity class, the stars of video, with millions of fans hungrily renting cassettes of his old movies. So it is appropriate that Selleck would want to protect his image, going so far as to sue. When a tabloid covered a story about a series of posters which had been slapped on hundreds of empty spaces in New York City by a group called Outpost, one of which identified the "Magnum P.I." hunk as "gay," they printed the poster with the headline, "'Gay' Stars Stop Traffic." Said the star: "There is not a man who has lived on the face of the Earth in my lifetime who can truthfully deny what is so obviously my choice: that is, that I am singularly heterosexual." He went on to say the story had made him subject of "hatred, contempt, ridicule and obloquy." The tabloid's editor Wendy Henry said the article was "a news report of a perfectly factual story." Later she was to say, "The story did not intend to express or imply that Tom Selleck is or ever was homosexual." The judge disagreed, awarding damages to Selleck.

The *National Enquirer* got in the act by claiming that country heartthrob Randy Travis was gay. "I usually let things slide but I couldn't this time," Travis said. "Someone in Nashville is quoted as saying 'if Randy Travis isn't gay, then my grandmother is Willie Nelson.' The person that made that statement better tell his grandmother to buy a red wig, get a bandanna and learn to sing through her nose. There's not a man alive that can prove I'm gay." Maybe he fucked 'em all to death? Oh, and don't forget, Joan Rivers said she's seen Travis' furniture and she knows he couldn't be gay!

Another "Absolutely Queer" victim was Presidential son Ron Reagan, who comes across as a basically decent person with nimble wit who tried to make a success as a latenight talk show host. In one episode about AIDS, an angry man in the audience accused Ron, who has been married for 11 years, of being a "liar" for denying he was gay. "Do you know me?" Ron snapped. "Have we ever met? Then where do you get off calling me a liar? Come on, you don't know anything." The show's original 11:30 p.m. time slot was supposed to reflect its younger, hipper target audience, but the experiment in scheduling daytime fluff at night proved to be a disaster as the program was rescheduled to the nether regions of the morning. Critic Mike Rubin commented: "Reagan is too smug and flip, coming on like a grad student on speed, but as a subtext to the last decade, he never ceases to amaze. Too bad Junior is more successful as an unknown thorn in his Pop's side than as a plumber of the zeitgeist."

Someone who does know something is Barbra Streisand. She knows a good thing when she sees it, especially if someone else points it out. Many actors were considered for the part of Bernard Lowenstein, psychiatrist Susan Lowenstein's adolescent son in "Prince of Tides," but there was difficulty finding the right one. Author Pat Conroy noticed a picture of the star's son Jason on her desk and exclaimed, "That's Bernard!" He was able to convince her that her son would be perfect casting as her son. This is the same boy that the *London Sun* had claimed had married his male underwear modelling boyfriend. The *New York Daily News* howled: "Barbra's got her Flatbush up over this!" Said the star: "I am thoroughly disgusted that my son is now being attacked with cruel and vicious lies." But all of the guests were listed by name and, as Michael Musto said in *The Village Voice*, "The guy's gorgeous so Barbra should get over herself. I'm surprised she's in such a tizzy. Last year, she was on the set trying to teach Jason how to walk less mincingly." Mama said, "My kid's a perfectionist, like me. And he really wanted to play it." This is a boy who Barbra says is not very ambitious and has never asked for anything in his whole life, except perhaps to be left alone to marry his boyfriend.

Speaking of boyfriends, or the lack thereof, comic actress Lily Tomlin's always kept 'em guessing but in an appearance at the L.A. Hilton to benefit the Gay and Lesbian Center she was remarkably open. In an Ernestine routine, she fielded queer-related calls to the Center and then, as herself, announced, "Congratulations to all of us for 20 years of being gay." As Michael Musto said, "All of us? Lily capped the show by doing an elaborate tango with a woman and the star-studded audience went dizzy from these sudden signs of intelligent life."

In another interview, Lily said she was an artist first and she didn't want to make her art propagandistic. The reason, she feels, more entertainers don't come out is "they wouldn't get certain parts. If it's too widely known, people will project that the audience is making those projections. It's not like someone's sexuality is not known (within the industry) in most instances. In what seem to be the most obvious examples, I don't think anyone in the industry is in the dark. Some people have a sense of privacy they don't want violated. There are a lot of people who do it and don't have to take on the world. It's one thing to protect yourself in a phony way and another thing..." She trailed off. Finally, she said, "I've been a public person for 20 years and I've never dated boys. Whenever I see an outing list it's so damn short. If there were a significant number of people...but there isn't enough to make a difference."

Writer Roger Evans disagrees: "The right to privacy has to yield to the greater need of bringing closeted politicians, actors and media people out into the real world. It is just no longer acceptable for covert homosexuals to oppose gay rights and continue living the lie. And the Hollywood actors and media people who reinforce homophobia and the myth of 'normal' sexuality should all be pulled in. Their hypocrisy has blocked funds for AIDS, obstructed reforms and continued the opppression of gay men and women. Having been dragged out of the closet, these powerful, privileged men and women will now have to face the same problems and dilemmas of ordinary unprotected mortals. It will be a shock. They will have to search for new personal identities and relationships and fight the same battles as most other lesbians and gay men." Especially the young, who gay writer Michael Dregni says are being discouraged from claiming their sexual identity when faced with growing homophobia, disease and death. This will only mean a growth in closeted gay behavior and greater incidences of unsafe sex and sexual harassment may result, making it riskier for gays and straights alike.

Brad Davis, the hunky star of "Midnight Express" and "Querelle," hid his HIV-positive status from Hollywood elite for six years, fearing he'd never work again. After the huge success of "Express," Brad said he became an addict and "was sexually very promiscuous." Real stardom eluded him because he was known around town as a party boy out of control and he didn't mind taking risky roles, even playing a gay. But even when he dried out, he couldn't get the top roles. Then the power elite in Hollywood became even more AIDSphobic than homophobic, if that's possible.

It's no wonder that, as the years pass, one needs a scorecard to keep up. I have taken the liberty of refining Musto's current list of our favorite types of celebrities, in descending order: (1) the ones who say, "Yes I'm gay. What's it to you?" (Gus Van Sant, Terry Sweeney, Harvey Fierstein, Johnny Mathis); (b) are not gay, but say, "I'd love to try it!" (Roseanne Barr Arnold); (c) say "I'm bisexual" (David Geffen, Boy George, Elton John, Martina Navratilova); (d) "I've had gay/lesbian experiences" (Michelle Shocked, Madonna, Richard Chamberlain, even Brando); (e) say "I'm happy with my sexuality, whatever it is," (David Cassidy); (f) say, "I'm not gay, but I love gay people," (Richard Gere, Dolly Parton); (g) don't say anything (Jodie Foster); (h) say "I'm not gay," and immediately have a companion of the opposite sex (Whitney Houston, John Travolta); (i) claim to have no sexuality at all, take the Domestic Mischief Poster Child, 11-year-old Macaulay Caulkin on dates, then playfully unzip his pants and rub his crotch with the best of 'em: Black Panther wanna-be Michael Jackson.

Hollywood, according to many in the business, perpetuates its own idea of homosexuals. "We tend to be represented totally by stereotypes and as villains and that's why nothing ever changes," comments the best-selling novelist Paul Monette, who wrote a "thirtysomething" episode on AIDS. "If you have somebody like Eddie Murphy telling homophobic jokes all the time, you wonder why homophobia is like it is?"

Scott Robe, founder of Out in Film, an organization of homosexuals working in movies and TV, says, "Hollywood works on the premise that the American public is stupid. It thinks that if it provides an enlightened image of gays and lesbians as the people next door, Americans will turn off the set or stop buying tickets."

"It's true," Craig Lucas said. Referring to his film, "Longtime Companion," he commented, "It touched a nerve, suggesting that homosexuals aren't necessarily exotic. But the class of people who objected to the movie the most were the ones depicted in the movie."

We have met the enemy and it is us?

Book I.
Sex in Cinema

Keanu Reeves and River Phoenix, Photographed by Herb Ritts

Director Gus Van Sant: "Even when we did our scene - you know, when you were in the middle of it - it was tough to do."
Star River Phoenix: "Well, when it came down to it, we were just doing it. We were just like -"
GVS: "You're just trying to like - "
RP: "To fuck."
GVS: "Just to do it from the point of view of the partners involved in having sex. That's the way to get around it."

Sex In Cinema

"I try to become more like myself every day."
- Quentin Crisp in "Resident Alien."

The evening before the grand premiere of Jonathan Nossiter's film about Quentin Crisp, "Resident Alien," a party was held to celebrate at the famed New York disco Limelight. The subject of the film was carried into the room seated on a Roman-style chair by bikini clad musclemen, offering the crowd bottles of "Shy Violet" hair rinse...but let's let him tell about it in his own inimitable style: "The glamorous Lauren Hutton showered me with gifts and opened the show. What she said I have no idea, beause at the moment when she was addressing the multitude, I was hiding in a side entrance to the building with two magnificent gentlemen who were wearing costumes the size of Band-aids. (It was decided) that I should enter on a sedan chair. This was not a Queen Anne type of conveyance, a small cabinet with curtained doors on either side in whch, unseen by the vulgar mob, ladies of high degree could be carried through the streets by footmen somewhat more warmly dressed than my impressive assistants. No, the contraption on which I was transported was simply a chair with handles protruding fore and aft by means of which the two musclemen carried me into full view of the public. I was slightly unnerved by this ceremony but tried to laugh off my embarrassment."

"Resident Alein" is a successful follow-up to "The Naked Civil Servant," which starred John Hurt as Crisp (Hurt appears briefly along with Holly Woodlawn, Fran Lebowitz and Sting). Raved Bob Satuloff in *The New York Native*: "An appealing, sometimes disturbing portrait of the persona Crisp has forged and the life he has built since coming to the U.S."

Of course, the film is loaded with typical Crisp-isms: "By chance, I am gradually becoming a sort of tinted George Burns." (Tainted would be more like it.) "I do think of myself as artificial, as an invention." (You are what you are.) "In New York, you can do fame by itself. It can become a career." (He's done that, in spades.) "I have come to represent a sad person's view of a gay person." (So let 'em be sad.)

To coincide with the film's release, Crisp was caught up in a publicity fever and besides going to parties, he was granting interviews like mad. Said he: "Nearly all interviews consist largely of an attempt to present my early life as a perfumed fist being shaken in the face of British narrow-mindedness -an interpretation which I always try to correct by explaining that in fact I was a helpless victim of my nature pleading with the world to forgive my difference from it.

"I do not scour each day's papers and magazines for reviews of any of my performances (but I do read some and) would like to express a faint bewilderment at the often voiced description of me as 'opaque.' As far as I know, I have never given any evasive reply to any question about my ideas or events in my life. My responses are aphoristic, not in order to conceal my meaning, but because they have been made so often that they have become crystalized, if not fossilized. Criticism of 'Resident Alien' seems to be in the same vein; it is said to reveal nothing new about me. How can it? It is sometimes compared unfavorably to 'The Naked Civil Servant.' That was completed when I was already sixty-six, long past the age when I could be overtaken by any major change other than decay. It was never my place to ask Mr. Nossiter what his intention was in making the film. I merely presumed it was an attempt to depict my life in America, to show how far it has fulfilled my dream of it, and to allow some denizens of the Lower East Side to express their opinions of me."

Whatever those opinions may be, the release of "Alien" capped an intriguing year for gays on film. "The love that dare not speak its name" is always a risky business for even foreign filmmakers, but challenging new works held sway at film festivals and large city arthouses, making us salivate at the thought of the potential video releases. Many complained of the "images" presented in the year's crop but, as the late critic Vito Russo always maintained, "judging the gay content of art should never be a case of whether the presentation is 'good for gay people.' It's never that simple. I always try to take into account the apparent intent of the artist as well as the context in which lesbians or gay men are presented."

While "Resident Alien" showed us somebody happy with being gay, leave it to a gay filmmaker to show us the underbelly, the lowlife aspect that would certainly be acceptable to anybody who ever wanted to condemn homosexuals.

While it's fun to see beautiful boys playing at being gay in "My Own Private Idaho," the latest in Gus Van Sant's excursions on the wild side of the street, starring teen idols Keanu Reeves and River Phoenix as hustlers in Portland, it's bothersome to some gays that this is the only kind of depiction Hollywood will allow. One wag suggested that they should have taken advantage of the boys' popularity and called it "Bill and Ted's Excellent Homo Adventure" or "Stand By Me While I Cruise." Another said, "Reeves is a slumming straight boy, Phoenix is a narcoleptic; otherwise, they are just your usual Hollywood hunks."

When his first film, 1985's "Mala Noche," was named the Best Independent/Experimental Film by the Los Angeles Film Critics Association (also made in Portland and on a budget of only $20,000) Van Sant's reputation was made. The film, a memoir of Portland poet and streetperson Walt Curtis, was described by the filmmaker as "'Death in Venice' on skid row." It was a touching story of the taunting of a convenience store clerk by a migrant worker. "The book is pornographic," Gus says. "It talks about what it feels like to stick your dick up someone's butt, and it feels like chocolate up there. Emotionally the book worked but it was hard in the film to get as far as Walt did with his language." In the love scenes, Gus decided not to show anything, just hint at it and, instead of playing beautiful music, he plays up reality.

The director's next film, "Drugstore Cowboy," featuring a stunning performance by Matt Dillon as a junkie, got uniformly fine reviews and did good business, enabling the filmmaker to get financing for "Idaho," even though, as he says, it's anticommercial by today's Hollywood standards: "It is like an inch away from being a mainstream, commercial movie. Not like a mile. It's not hard to take. It just shows you how stodgy, conservative and afraid Hollywood is today to even consider a project that isn't like 'Home Alone.' You only go this far away and everybody thinks Keanu and River are playing with fire. I think they're just bored with what they do."

Playboy magazine's Bruce Williamson enjoyed "Idaho:" "There are two movies here that Van Sant never quite brings together, nor does he address anything so realistic as the menace of AIDS. But as a nonjudgmental study of human frailty, 'Idaho' is bold, risky and disarming."

David Handelman in *Rolling Stone* also raved : "...what makes them good are the nonverbal elements: Van Sant's dry wit, painter's eye, musician's ear (he once fronted a band called Destroy All Blondes), his openness to improvisation and his anything-goes sensibility."

That "anything-goes sensibility" appealed to his young actors. One tabloid even insinuated Keanu went "way into" his role by "shacking up with drug-using streetfolk." But this wasn't really true, according to the star. Drugs were really not part of the scene. Says Keanu: "We smoked weed once in a while, sipped some red wine."

"I was encouraging my people to understand the life, not live it," Gus comments. "I don't know anything about shooting up in my house. I wasn't party to it if it happened." Further, he professes not to know how the streets work today. And, in fact, he says, "I'd rather hang out with straight guys and not get sex than to hang out with gay guys." However, back in the '70s when he was working at Paramount, Gus did hang out with gay guys, on Santa Monica Boulevard at the Gold Cup Cafe. He read John Rechy's "City of Night" and became interested in the lives of hustlers. "And I guess," he says, "sex for sale is just an intriguing subject." Today, however, those streets have become mean. "If we went to the street, you'd find that out right away. We'd probably get mugged or something." Now he says he's "the kind of person that just makes it up at home. I mean, certain people who lived that life were around during filming. It's like if you're making a film about boating, you have some boaters around or else a storm's gonna come up and drown you. But half the time, you're right anyway." Having also lived in New York, he knows something about the scene there as well. And he says that the New Yorkers are a lot cuter than what he found in Hollywood. The Portland boys, on the other hand, are a different breed altogether: "They're nicer. It's more like an old time honky-tonk existence as opposed to a hardcore one. There have always been drugs, but modern drugs really changed the face of that kind of life. Especially Santa Monica Boulevard...and some of the kids who were in the movie described Polk Street as, like, rat-infested. There are desperate characters here, but the guys

I've known haven't been like that. They're like lifers - it's a job to them. They get up and go to work every day and come home."

While *Newsweek* reported that Gus was "openly gay," and he does have a longtime boyfriend from Rotterdam, he prefers not to discuss his private life. "Your sexuality is a private thing and as far as culture goes, I don't think of a gay culture separate from a mass culture. I just look at it as human culture. I mean, it's obvious that there's all kinds of stuff oriented toward heterosexual culture, because that's the majority, but it's also oriented towards white culture because that's the majority. It's not surprising and it doesn't bother me.

"Inside certain other cultures, artistic ones, a lot of friends of mine that are straight feel left out, because the major composers and artists of this century are gay. They feel inferior, to the point where they wish they were gay. So it depends on what group you want to join. I've never had any trouble in Hollywood because I don't push anything on people, so it's never been hard on me. My lifestyle isn't even a particularly gay lifestyle. I'm just an artist-bachelor type. My crowd is just weirdos."

Gus says the street scene portrayed in the movie no longer even exists, quashed by urban renewal and the threat of AIDS. The street hustlers have moved on to other venues, most of the porn theaters are shut down and the block is dominated by a sleek new Justice Center.

But the Video Follies store, where River emerges from the covers of porn magazines, is still there and the star and Gus re-visited the scene. Inside, the place had changed. "You filmed just in time," the attendant said. "There's new owners now; they want a more boutiquey kind of thing. Now it's just a generic smut shop - though it still has vestiges of its former self. Everywhere you look it's - ugh!"

"I couldn't look anywhere," River said.

"You can't stay in there too long," Gus agreed, and they left.

Thirty-nine-year-old Van Sant takes time out every year to make a short film and this year it was "Five Naked Boys With a Gun," featuring young men between the ages of 19 and 26 who wrestle each other for the control of a gun. Shot in black and white and slow motion, it will run three minutes after editing. (River commented that he would have been in the short except that he was "busy" with making "Idaho." Talk about missed opportunities!)

Gay stereotypes held sway in other films during the year, including the thriller, "Silence of the Lambs," wherein a mincing, lipstick-and-wig-wearing, poddle-kissing young man is a woman-skinning serial killer. And then there was the narcissistic psycho in "The Hard Way" who covered his face in masque and gets off watching himself dance half-naked in a mirror. And Blake Edwards doesn't seem to think audiences will buy gays who don't wear high-heels and mascara. After "Victor/Victoria," he did it again in "Switch," without the same hilarious results. Enough already.

Gay stereotypes of another kind came to national attention with the release of "Poison," showing gay sex in a prison setting, inspired by "Miracle of the Rose" by Jean Genet (who, in "Thief's Journal," wrote, "The most sordid signs become for me the signs of grandeur."). Although this was only one of three segments of this feature, for which postproduction costs were funded with $25,000 of our tax dollars through the National Endowment for the Arts, it is the most powerful one and was the cause for all the uproar. Thirty-year-old filmmaker Todd Haynes quickly moved into the ranks of cult celebrity and found Hollywood knocking on his door. Tall, blond and cute San Fernando Valley boy Todd finds labeling his film as "gay," shocking. He disdains labels of any kind, finding them annoyingly reductive and dismissive. "It's a complicated issue, because words only clumsily express what we feel. I think it's extremely important for gay sensibilities to be discussed openly. We're looking at the status quo from a skewed perspective -whereas films like 'Making Love, 'Cruising,' and 'Longtime Companion' were incredibly straight; they were conveniently created."

Haynes admits, however, than anyone expecting gratuitous titillation is likely to come away from "Poison" disappointed. "I never thought of it as a crossover film. I just wanted to make a film on my own terms. I wanted it to be sexy. But after this flap, people are going to expect more."

He was delighted, however, when straights found the film sexy. "Women really find it sexy and I think straight men do, but they don't have as easy a time admitting it. I think that's good. I think gay people can look at straight films and get turned on for all kinds of reasons and straight people can look at gay films and get turned on for all kinds of reasons. That's part of it, not being afraid of being attracted to these phantoms on the wall that are playing out their desires in ways that are going to touch you now and then."

According to Haynes (whom one critic dubbed as "the new whiz kid on the outlaw movie block" and another called "subversively gifted"): "Genet was the genesis of 'Poison.' The model of Genet: the artist who is involved in the subject but refuses to be taken in by it. Genet questions my own involvement in the status quo. He also questions my involvement in the gay world which is now stigmatized as the world of AIDS." Haynes questions the desire for some gays to "clean up their acts," to remove the trangression from being gay. "This prompted me to want to delve into that world even more. 'Poison' is a look at transgression through different means. ...The film is so much about exclusion. I had to choose certain subjects to make central. Genet's characters were invariably white and not faggy; he was idealizing the source of oppression. I wanted to create a work that, while raising those issues, was an experience that transformed, and was transcendental. What's more interesting is the experience of trying to transform. We take what society considers ugly and make it beautiful."

The "beautiful" scene during which so many patrons walked out involved a group of reform school hellions who take turns spitting into a boy's mouth. A similar scene in "Taxi Zum Klo," in which a man urinates in another's mouth, is much more to the point and didn't cause much fuss, probably because it wasn't funded by the N.E.A. Critic J. Hoberman called the sequence "a lush pastiche of Genet's 'Miracle of the Rose,' it details a doomed and brutal prison romance, replete with flashbacks to an incongruously bucolic Borstal, whose rosy light and overgrown foliage suggest a pleasure garden out of Watteau."

Indeed, Hoberman notes, from Kenneth Anger's "Fireworks" on, "American avant-garde cinema has been richly informed by homosexual sensibility and subject matter. No film has ever taken this more for granted than 'Poison.'"

The showbiz bible *Variety* said: "Done is earnest, the 'Homo' sequence will throw more than a few unsuspecting viewers. A mood of seething violent homoeroticism permeates the proceedings as one prisoner stalks another in an episode spiked with multiple glimpses of rear-entry intercourse and one of genital fondling. But the most explicit and sure to be talked-about scene is a flashback in which several young men humiliate another by repeatedly spitting into his gaping mouth."

Critic David Ehrenstein was downright touched that "19 years after Divine ate doggie shit in 'Pink Flamingos,' it's possible to do something that upsets people!"

Director Haynes admitted: "There is genital fondling, mostly through the pants. You get a very quick glimpse of a penis in it. And that's it. There is a rape at the end of the film, which is basically covered by a medium two-shot of two inmates, focusing on their heads. There are two cutaways to their pants, but all you see is one-half of a guy's thigh, and mostly a lot of clothing hanging off. It's very tasteful." (And not nearly as arousing as Racquel Welch's rape of the bodybuilder in "Myra Breckenridge.")

A critic for *The Los Angeles Times* said: "This is Genet as done by Eagle Scout troop No. 17, a very peculiar business."

But *Rolling Stone* was hardly shocked. It grumbled, "This faux-arty exercise in self-indulgence won the Grand Jury Prize at the 1991 Sundance Film Festival. Perhaps the judges bought the publicity handed out by Haynes...The film plays like a student thesis. Neither witty, lyric nor shocking enough to have an impact. At least it's consistent: it's badly written, acted and directed."

Bob Satuloff said: "'Poison' unapologetically presents homosexuals as the shunned, the criminal, the perversely poetic, the intrinsically dangerous. Whether or not one agrees with or approves of this view seems less relevant than the fact that it was destined to be expressed sooner or later. It might be expected that a film this extreme would be identified within the industry as one capable of attracting only the smallest possible audience segment, a cult within a cult within a cult...It's often grim, paced in a measured dreamlike way. It's not an easily accessible piece of filmmaking, and its sexual politics are, at the very least questionable. Yet...the movie confronts the viewer with images that won't easily go away. 'Poison' exerts a degree of power that one rarely comes across these days."

Newsweek agreed: "'Poison doesn't go down easy, and it isn't meant to. But we should thank the NEA, not curse them, for helping it on its way."

The government's arts czar, N.E.A. Chairman John Frohmayer,

said: "Taken as a whole, the film illustrates the effect of violence...It is the work of a serious artist dealing with serious issues in our society. It is neither purient or obscene."

Another film made by a serious artist during the year that attracted the attention of gay critics was "Young Soul Rebels," from Isaac Julien, the director of the widely-praised 45-minute documentary about bisexual poet Langston Hughes, "Looking for Langston." Critic Georgia Brown said the film was much harsher visually, with all the seams showing, "but also setting out to show how black and gay, as well as black and white, and gay and straight, might coexist." The quasi-autobiographical story of what it was like for the director being 17 in the year 1977 carries an opening suggestion that gay sex - and black-white sex - is potentially lethal, and proceeds to present a "Blow-Up"-style murder mystery. As Brown commented, "The movie is so engaging, so friendly really, that weaknesses can seem part of the charm." Julien's lover of four years, Mark Nash, is white and also a filmmaker, working on a lesbian-themed movie to be called "Memoirs of a Space Woman." "It's our own gay community," Julien says, "that's come up with the most derogatory terms to describe black men who are attracted to white men, they're called 'snow queens.' And the white men who are attracted to black men are called 'dinge queens.' So what does that say about the gay community?"

The film's most beautiful scene occurs when the lovers go to bed. Critic David Ehrenstein says, "Performing with gusto, the lovers in this scene, which is tender, touching and erotic all at the same time, go far beyond the feverish clinches seen in 'My Beautiful Launderette.'"

Some in the audience are bound to be horrified at this interracial sex scene, but, as Ehrenstein points out, "in scratching at this raw social nerve, (the film) shows how the personal can become political in a new and challenging way. This British film may deal with young black people and the pop music scene much as any commercial American film would, but it does so with a political slant. And the crux of that politics is gay." Julien says he would like to see more of the recognition of the differences in the cultures than the erasing of those differences. "Political correctness can be boring," he says. "I'm not out to prove my blackness to blacks - or whites." The film won the Critics Week Prize at the Cannes Film

Festival.

During the year, one was hard pressed to find a movie with flattering gay characters, but there were some demonstrating gays working their way through it and these were documentaries: "Kush," about lesbians and gays in India, and the unquestioned hit of the year, "Paris Is Burning." Happy being gay? Well, no, not really, but how about happy vogueing? "Paris Is Burning" was celebrated at the Whitney Biennial exhibit and one reviewer raved, "It's on my (and everybody else's) top-10 list and by far the most powerful film about race on the program." About race, get it?

A film by Jennie Livingston, "Paris" shows "a culture far more complex than the familiar image of dancers flailing around pretending to be snooty runway models," according to critic Jim Farber. The film depicts vogueing from Harlem drag balls of the twenties through today's events, which offer endless competitive categories, such as "Butch queen in drag," "Looking like a girl going to school," or even "Looking like a boy that probably robbed you a few minutes before you came in." The personality overhauls of the dancers give the balls a subversive edge, stressing the sly mutability of identity. That's the angle that first attracted Livingston when she was taking film classes at NYU in 1985. Says she: "I'd always been interested in issues of race, class and gender and it seemed to me the vogueing balls were an amazing repository of ideas on all these issues. The ball world explores how you fit into society. It's about how gay people have to try to pass as straight people in society. Even straight men or women in society have to pass as real men or real women." She says that although the film covers the graphic, sometimes depressing aspects of voguers' lives, theft, prostitution, and homophobic murders, it never panders to its subjects. It merely shows the hopes and dreams of people expressing themselves and dealing with the reality of society. "When you don't have the opportunities others have, you make do -and that's what the whole ball culture is really about."

The film is a marvelous testimony to the fact that self-expression cannot be killed. No matter what limitations people suffer, they will find means to speak, ways to speak. Forced by their preferences to exist on the fringes of society, they've given up conventional dignity in order to survive. They've replaced it with an alternative dignity, which finds expression in posing and dancing like magazine models, hence the name "vogueing." The result, on screen, is not for the prudish or squeamish.

"It's ironic," Livingston notes, "that ball people re-create a society that hates them, but perhaps even more ironic that in the end, when Madonna made vogueing such a big thing, society imitated the ball people."

In sum, says the filmmaker, "These are people taking a rough situation and turning it into humor and expression." The filmmaker herself, among them. To make the movie she walked the streets of Harlem at all hours of the day and night. One time a black dude approached her and asked, "Are you for real?" "No," she replied.

"What makes all of this indelible is the people we meet," commented *Entertainment Weekly*. "The funny and self-mocking 'legend' Pepper LeBeija (who says, "I've been a man and I've been a man who emulated a woman. I've never been a woman."); the supermodel wannabe Octavia Saint Laurent, who flashes a ravishing smile; and, most hauntingly, the innocent and sultry teen prostitute Venus Xtravaganza, who, with his doomed dreams of middle-class bliss (and of finally getting a sex change) is like a Dickensian waif turned into a surreal emblem of late 20th-century yearning." Says the character, "I never felt comfortable being poor, or even middle class doesn't suit me."

Critic David Denby: "It's the opposite of camp and finally heartbreaking in its longing for the power to be oneself, a power that most of us take for ranted."

To come full circle, Quentin Crisp said: "A startling mixture of the bizarre and the heart-breaking. A fascinating picture." *The New Yorker's* Terrence Rafferty said, "Every man we meet in this picture is the product of a tireless, fanatically scrupulous art practiced on himself - each man his own Pygmalion and his own Galatea...There's no accounting for this sort of theatrical transport. It is, perhaps, a joy that only the most abandoned of performers will ever know, and all we can do is gaze on it, in delight and awe; its sources are beyond the reach of our formulations."

"(The film) has become a big hit in Chicago," reported Preston Guider, "with full house crowds quoting lines ("Rocky Horror Picture Show"-style) along with the actors on screen. Looks like we have our own cult classic movie now. The question is not whether you've seen it but how many times."

There were other movies you wouldn't want to see once, let alone twice, even some with supposed homoerotic content, if reviewers could be believed. But as Satuloff says, "I've come to the conclusion that when a movie is called homoerotic, the most you can assume is that there are men in it. Whatever else one's radar happens to pick up, as with beauty, exists pretty much in the eyes and mind of the beholder. Critics have always had a field day sniffing out homoeroticism in 'Rebel Without a Cause,' 'Red River,' and all sorts of stuff both likely and unlikely, from any World War II combat actioner you'd care to name all the way to 'King Kong' (which, according to a friend of mine, is clearly a parable of male sexual jealousy). The subject is a vertiable minefield, with lots of confused people dazedly staggering through it, a good many of them picking up Ph.D.s and getting published for their trouble.

"Very often, gay men respond to films in which men care for each other, express their affection, movies in which brothers, fathers and sons, or same-sex friends love one another deeply and aren't afraid to show it, but they can hardly be considered homoerotic. What we're talking about here is the acting out of unacknowledged sexuality, barely disguised: the villain who looks as if he'd just as soon have his way with the hero between the sheets or pump him full of holes; the hero whose hatred of the villain is too passionate and obsessive to accept at face value; characters of equal weight shown in contrast; men at odds."

Speaking of being at odds, we prefer boys at odds and for a chickenhawk's money you couldn't get more homoerotic than "Toy Soldiers," now out on video. Satuloff dubbed the film "Briefs Encounters," given the director's penchant for displaying its young male cast in all manner of underwear: "These prep school boys take their clothes off at the drop of a hat, and the camera is right there to record every juxtaposition of cotton fabric - in a wide range of designer colors - against young flesh. While not particularly steamy, this unending fashion parade is presumably aimed at the market segment perceived to be the film's target audience: adolescent girls in mall miniplexes." And us chickenhawks. In this little movie we find Sean Astin (of "War of the Roses" and "Memphis Belle") and Wil Wheaton (who was so adorable in "Stand By Me," the TV series "Star Trek: The Next Generation," and who also popped up in a TV movie during the year called "The Last Prostitute") in what Satuloff said was a mediocre film that could have been "wonderfully, excruciatingly bad." But you can't have everything.

While some reviewers found it "homoerotic," Satuloff found "The Killer" having absolutely zero such content. Perhaps those reviewers saw something in the fact that the two leads are, at the end, shoulder to shoulder "blasting one battalion of baddies after another inside a Catholic church."

For our money, "Queens Logic" had enough homoeroticism to make up for its other shortcomings, thanks to an alert cameraman. This movie is all about living in New York's borough of Queens, not about queens, but it does have a very uptight gay character, played by John Malkovich, who at one point bemoans the fact that "I'm a homosexual who can't relate to gay men." He is just one of a bunch of guys growing up but struggling mightily not to mature, and, by the fadeout, he does meet a sensitive young man who seems to "make his day." But what we enjoyed most about this rambling trifle was co-star Kevin Bacon (a chickenhawk's wet dream in "Footloose") returning to his dancing roots, this time writhing on his back on the dance floor in some very tight orange pants. Blessedly, the cameraman lingered lovingly on the crotch area for several moments and we could rewind it, then play it in slow motion for maximum effect.

And it was a year when, in "Sheltering Sky," we are treated to a nice close up glimpse of John Malkovich's cock.

Yes, it was a year when you had to be thankful for small favors.

Movie Stars:
The Best of the Fantasy Lovers

"Rudolph Valentino was not just another movie star," notes historian Richard Koszarski of the American Museum of the Moving Image. "He was a one-man cultural phenomenon who shattered his audience's long accepted notions of male sexuality." Before Valentino, the popular male stars were Douglas Fairbanks, Harold Lockwood and Wallace Reid, handsome but hardly sexy; the kind of guys girls would be proud to bring home to meet Mom. Valentino was something else entirely. He was an openly sexual icon designed to feed the most hidden fantasies of the cinema's largely female audience, to say nothing of the gaymale. Traditional values were trashed when he appeared on screen, hinting of violent sexuality and miscegenation.

Years ago, Miriam Hansen challenged the prevailing assumptions of feminist film scholarship by arguing that Valentino's vehicles were the first movies to recognize female spectatorship as a mass phenomenon. The fact that women were fascinated by Valentino despite the widespread contempt of male authorities (who regarded him as perverse or worse) prompts Hansen to conclude that Valentino's films articulate a desire outside motherhood or the family. Valentino was attacked as unmanly (variously rumored to be homosexual, impotent, masochistic, dominated by lesbians) because he posed a threat, not a threat merely of sexual difference but, as Hansen puts it, of a "different kind of sexuality."

Valentino opened the door for a pantheon of sexy male actors and each year new ones emerge, some to flicker only briefly, others to begin building substantial careers, beguiling gaymales as they grow older and some even sexier before our eyes.

When it comes to beauty, notwithstanding the vagaries of individual taste, occasionally boys come along who were meant, like the bands on a coral snake or the face of the Matterhorn, to showcase what Mother Nature really intended. And nobody responds more than gaymales, who embrace these present and future icons, finding in them the eternal hope of possibility. The sex stars become safe harbor on a stormy night and, in our fantasies, we can make them do anything we want.

Because variety is the spice of life, you are often stunned with the multiplicity of choices. As the actress Sandra Bernhard succinctly puts it, "One man, however splendid, simply cannot meet all your needs. That is why the search continues, but never in vain. They all give me a gift that has enriched my soul, changing me forever."

River Phoenix

Once there was a boy who was so adorable you couldn't keep your eyes off him. The movie was "Mosquito Coast" and the only thing wrong about it was that this kid was so young. Then, released in the same year, 1986, came "Stand By Me." Could this kid be for real? It wasn't until "A Night with Jimmy Reardon," when he was at last having sex, that you decided, quite firmly, that "a night with River Phoenix" would surely be one of the most splendid of your life.

Oh, from everything you'd heard, this kid was different. In person, you kept thinking, you'd probably change your mind in a hurry. But the fantasy persisted because, given the lad's penchant for doing his own thing, there was the faint hope that you could get him to see things from your perspective.

And then, speaking of doing his own thing, came "My Private Idaho." Teen idol Keanu Reeves' agent was amenable to his being part of the project but Phoenix's agent flatly refused to even show his client the script. Famed gay director Gus Van Sant smuggled River a copy and the young star took over a month to think about it, but he committed to the difficult part as the homeless male hustler. "Keanu and I made a blood brother pact," River says. "Anyone who has a problem, fuck 'em. That's all I can say. A big capital F and a U-C-K, and then THEM. I get negative shit all the time. I don't care."

River, if you don't care, neither do we. Bless him, he kept the fantasy alive. "In society there's this confusion between love and sex," the boy says. "People think they want love and that they'll get it through sex. Very rarely do the two merge cohesively. The character I play is very clear on the difference between love and sex, because he has sex for a living. That's why his line was so important (in the big scene he does with Keanu). 'I love you, and you don't pay me.' I wrote that line. I'm glad I wrote that line. They tell me nobody's ever said that before on screen. I'm so proud. That's great! Cool! We're movin' along."

(Movin' along indeed. Keep it up, Riv!)

"Being that homophobia is like a religion, I don't know that there's going to be that much space in the marketplace for this stuff. This helps it, though, get underway."

(There you go! Nice, Riv, really nice.)

And River's only 21. That's the most important thing about him. He's been in the movies so long, you'd think he was much older and he's even already been nominated for an Academy Award (for his poignant performance in "Running on Empty").

Born in a log cabin in Madras, Oregon, as a child River travelled with his parents to South America, then returned stateside in 1978, settling in Florida. He came to Los Angeles when he was 9. The star recalls: "I did my first work when I was 10. I did commercials and I did my first TV pilot that turned into a series when I was 11. That was 'Seven Brides for Seven Brothers.'" He appeared in "Robert Kennedy and His Times" and "Celebrity," both miniseries. In the latter he plays the part of a boy whose father is gay and he walks in on the lovers. "Big dramatic scene," River says. His debut film was "The Explorers," in 1985.

"Idaho" producer Laurie Parker recalls, "Making the movie was like the 'Attack of the Cute Boys.' We had lots of fun. In Italy, we stayed on a farm and became friends with our hosts. They wanted us to take this huge Romano cheese back to Hollywood. It was like they wanted that cheese to see Hollywood and Vine. The boys told them they'd make sure it got to the New World. That cheered them up."

Speaking of cheese, Van Sant had to assure the producers there'd be no "pickle shots," Hollywood's term for exposing the male sex organ. One executive cried, "If he's going to show erect dicks, I don't know what we're going to do!" Van Sant says, "Of course, it's only a problem because men get embarrassed when they see dicks on the screen. We needed to get an R-rating, that was in the contract. If I had complete freedom, it might have been different."

(One could only imagine what it would have been if River and Keanu had been able to expose themselves with full frontals...gasp

gasp.)

So we have to make do with River in a g-string. Gay writer Lance Loud described the scene: "Draped seminude over a rough-hewn cross, his hairless body drenched in golden light and his loincloth bulging with the help of foam-rubber padding, River Phoenix is posing for the cover a magazine called, 'G-String Jesus.'"

And we get the two boys with actor Udo Kier in a three-way which is filmed in a series of tasteful tableaux that change too quickly to tell who's doing what to whom, so one can only fantasize until we get the video and can freeze frame and study it closer. And then there's the moment when Keanu idly plays with River's tit while taunting police officers who are afraid to do anything to Keanu's character, the mayor's son.

Van Sant says that River's character may be gay but you're not really sure because he's not really sure. He says, "The hustlers and johns don't think of themselves as gay. In real life, the clients for these street hustlers tend to be middle class businessmen or construction workers with families."

River agrees: "There are a lot of street hustlers who are 'straight' who, to make money, do whatever they have to do. And then there are people who are part of the street gay life, who enjoy that, and that's their life. Mike, my character, is from the first group. He does it just for money. He's not part of that whole scene, which doesn't change anything, really, it's all the same scene, but that's how their psychology works. That's how they justify what they do." By observing the scene, River says he learned a lot: "I learned the importance of home. What he (the character Mike) doesn't have, I feel very lucky to have. It made me rethink what I have going for me."

Van Sant said, "Mike is sort of an embryo and I think River was playing it like that. He was doing things that I didn't even know he was doing. You only get to see Mike having pleasure when he hugs the guy at the end...in that scene where he watches 'The Simpsons.' He was supposed to hug the guy like it was something he lost that he needed very badly. He did it only once, it's true, but it was one of the main ideas behind his hustling, that he needed to be held, and touched. He didn't necessarily need to have sex. But he needed to be close. We didn't really explore that, except in that one little detail, which is really too bad, because it sort of was one of the inspirations for the whole film, the emotional breakdown in the mind of a street hustler. In this particular character, one of the main things he had was his need to be wanted, and he could be wanted by men who wanted him for various reasons, slightly different reasons than he wanted them to want him. He was really after attention and affection. But still what he missed was basically from a man, and not from a woman. He didn't have a father."

River's performance won him the Best Actor Award at the Venice Film Festival and critics' raves. Critic Lawrence Frascella said that Van Sant discovered previously unimagined depths in both of his stars, especially Phoenix. "I doubt there has ever been a screen character who embodies such fragility, helplessness, and defenselessness. A deeply moving experience. You don't need a film degree to appreciate it. Just an open mind." David Denby wrote: "Mike works the street and sells himself to men and occasionally to women. An aimless young dish, passive, not too bright, he doesn't have a mean bone in his pretty body. Like Myshkin's epilepsy in Dostoevski's 'The Idiot,' his narcolepsy is meant to be a sign of his essential innocence, more a poetic than a medical reality. River Phoenix is blond and smooth, and his face, softened with erotic pleasure and with sleep, is angelically empty. His Mike is like a dreamy piece of sculpture."*The New Yorker* cheered: "A superbly intelligent and intuitive performance." *Entertainment Weekly* found River's anonymous quality worked for him: "He gives an extraordinary performance." They found when he tells Keanu he wants to kiss him it is "the saddest, loneliest declaration of love imaginable."

When asked if there was any part of his relationship with Keanu on the screen, River said: "No, you'll never see that. That's the fun of what we do. It's a different world out there."

Wishing to remain far outside the Hollywood nexus of bad influences and superficial values, sauntering, wild-in-the-streets River's own world is a farm near Gainesville, Florida. He doesn't hang out with the students, though; mostly musicians, all terrifically polite, just like him. He's in a band, too, Aleka's Attic, and loves it, writing songs, singing songs, playing guitar. Island Records is interested in signing them, but River doesn't want people to come see the band just to see him.

And he doesn't get into the drug scene: "I just stay away from it.

It depresses me. The biggest thing that really gets me are the girls. Because of being used, the way men use women. It really upsets me. The wonderful extra-virgin-olive oil young ladies, who are so wholesome and together and their heads on straight and they get caught up and you see them a year later and they're - " he puts on a blank, empty face and round, blank eyes - "and all they've got left is just a recorded message in their heads. Nancy Reagan's said it all for me, 'Just say no.'"

When asked if he is a boy or a man, River replies: "I'm a lad." He wishes he'd waited to make love. "Yeah, I was four. With other kids. But I've blocked it out! I was completely celibate from ten to fourteen. I really haven't had sex with many people - five or six. I've just fallen into relationships that were fulfilling and easily monogamous. You know, that's the way it is: monogamy is monogamy until you screw someone else."

Another band member kidded River about his role: "Hey, I was waiting for you to kiss Keanu, there was such a build-up."

"But I didn't, man. You happy that I didn't? Don't you feel so much more comfortable being around me now, 'cause I'm a macho stud, right?"

"No, you're a wuss, Riv. Good shot of you guys pullin' up to town on the bike, though."

"Cool, huh? Was I studly enough for you?"

River maintains, "First of all, the picture's really not about gays. Second of all, I don't like have any real hang-ups."

What's next? River would like to do Shakespeare, with Keanu. Keanu says, "It'd be a hoot. We could do 'Romeo and Juliet.'"

"Yeah, " River says, "I'll be Juliet."

Keanu Reeves

Teen idol Keanu Reeves isn't too sure of what he's saying when he's asked to do an interview, a fact he's found quite funny while reading over some of his chats with members of the fourth estate. "I went through a self-conscious phase, 'cause I'm kinda goofy in real life," he says. "I'd read interviews I did and think, 'Wow! I'm a pretty goofy dude.' So I got over it and now I'm just hopeless."

We should all be so hopeless.

He's 27 but can look 17. "He has the look of jailbait," Sandra Bernhard says, " and that's damn sexy." His co-star in "Point Blank," Lori Petty says: "His innocence and charm are not contrived. He has an unintentional sexiness that keeps you off-balance. You don't know whether to play 'pillow talk' or 'tie me up, tie me down.'"

(Yummm. A little of each please.)

Keanu's exotic looks (his delicious lips, armpit, eyes and waist are featured in photographer Matthew Rolston's "Big Pictures," published by Little, Brown) are due to his bloodlines; he was born in Beirut, Lebanon, to an English mother and a father of Hawaiian-Chinese descent. His name means "cool breeze over mountains."

(Hmmm. Makes you want to just put your lips together and blow, doesn't it?)

Cool Keanu attended the High School for Performing Arts in Toronto but flunked out after a year. In Toronto, he appeared in a gay play called "Wolfboy," as, he says, "a jock who just lost it. He was under so much pressure he didn't know what was goin' on. Then he fell in love with this guy who gave him back his sense of power. And then he dumped this guy. And he killed me. Cut me. Sucked my blood!"

(Oh, when you're with Keanu there are so many things to suck, it makes one dizzy!)

Finally the actor broke into films in 1986 in Toronto as a goalie in the Rob Lowe plays-ice-hockey vehicle, "Youngblood," which led to Hollywood and memorable turns in "River's Edge," "Dangerous Liaisons," "I Love You to Death," "Tune in Tomorrow," and the goofy comedies of Bill and Ted.

As critic Chris Heath says, "He has instilled his characters with a rare sense of urgency and energy, and also with a beautiful, flawed honesty and naivete...an extraordinary actor, one who can project feelings onto film in a truly unusual way. He is somebody who has more than the right cheekbones, a rough 'n' ready demeanor, and puppy-dog eyes."

Adorable yes, but alas, a self-admitted airhead. The strapping 6', 170 lb. cutie calls himself "an ignorant pig:" "I'm makin' movies in Hollywood, you know? The things that I'm doin' are pretty sheltered. For me, acting is very self-involved, especially between projects. Once you get a part, you're liberated. You can find out what that character thinks."

While most young stars are paranoid about taking gay roles, Reeves took on the role of a mayor's son working the streets in "My Private Idaho" without giving it much thought. "I only have so much time. I might as well throw myself into the fire."

And rumors flew that he played with too much fire in his playing of the role, doing too many drugs with the real-life lowlifes hired to appear with him. When asked about it, the star shrugs and says, "I don't want to talk about it." What he does talk about is his part: "I play Scottie, who's based on Prince Hal from Shakespeare. I come from a wealthy background I've denied, been on the streets for three years. "

Cruising the streets is something Reeves knows lots about. Lately he's been cruising the boulevards on his bike. Says he: "L.A. is so trippy. Chhww. It becomes like a small town really quick. On those weekend nights the prostitutes are out, and the kids from school, and people cruising, and in the clubs all that stuff is going on. I ride my bike sometimes, just go out say around one and ride until four. Going downtown, riding around and just to look around. Goin' through the city to see who's doin' what where, you know?"

(Yeah, we know, Keanu. We know.)

When in New York, Keanu likes the Limelight. Michael Musto, reporting in *The Village Voice*: "He recently returned to the forbidden planet of Limelight and rather than drop trow, he lifted a girl's skirt, flirted with another and gave a guy his number - to be friends, OK? Everyone thrust drugs at him but (says one source) he stuck to a lilting mix of champagne and beer. At one point, he made guards clear a space on the dance floor for him to cavort in - another case of enforced celeb privacy in a public place."

Actually, Keanu seems to fear fame, as if it might sully everything, become a bother, mess up his freedom. What makes him happy, he says, is not fame but when he can get deeper into the fire and get better at being in it. He's not going to change the way he behaves for anyone. As for his sexuality, when best-selling author Dennis Cooper asked him if he was gay, he coyly replied, "No. But ya never know."

Hmmm. With answers like that, you recall how he prepared for a scene in "Idaho" by going into his hustler prowl and shouting,

"Hey! I know you want me. I know you want to do me. C'mon, suck my dick for money."

Okay, kid, just hold still for a second.

Jason Patric

We first were jolted into submission by the sight of Jason Patric in "Lost Boys," as the boy who would be Dracula. As Sandra Bernhard says, "Something in Patric's eyes makes me want to rescue him. Maybe I just have this sick thing for guys who like to get into accidents. But I know with Jason, nothing's an accident. And I also know that there are bad boys and then there are Lost Boys."

Then, the lost boy grew up in the film version of Jim Thompson's "After Dark, My Sweet," playing a slightly insane ex-boxer trying, not very successfully, to stay out of trouble. In his love scene with Rachel Ward we were treated to one of the most magnificent shots of a stud in action we're likely to see, bareass and all.

Raves a fan: "He's talented, handsome, serious, gorgeous, twisted, sexy and extremely intense. In other words, he has all the qualities of a superb actor."

Then he made headlines as the guy who took Julia Roberts away from Kiefer Sutherland (his co-star in "Lost Boys") and now he's playing a streetwise cop-turned-drug-addict in the $18-million project "Rush," starring opposite Jennifer Jason Leigh, who was so good in "Last Exit to Brooklyn." Jason got the plum role because director Lili Zanuck took her producer hubby Richard to the movies and couldn't get in to whatever it was they wanted to see so they bought tickets to "Sweet." When the movie was over they said, simultaneously, "That's the guy." Lili explains: "At some point in the past ten years, all our leading guys became boys. Jason's got an edge like a man. I haven't decided if I'm ever going to tell the truth about this Jason Patric thing...but maybe I just will. Jason was the very first actor that ever got this material. But he didn't commit to it right away because I was a first-time director. We sent it out to a couple of other people but told him, 'It's your part until it's cast.' Thank God he came back. He's the only actor under 30 who has a real edge. He's got a bit of that dangerous quality that was popular with leading men in the '50s."

Well, not all that dangerous. About the 26-year-old, who is Jackie Gleason's grandson, Jami Gertz, his co-star in "Boys," says, "He's very shy and introverted and it takes time and effort to find out who he is and how sweet and funny he is. And he's so manly. He taught me how to throw a football and play catch."

Just makes you want to ask Jason to teach you a little something, doesn't it?

Brad Pitt

In "Thelma and Louise," (a film Quentin Crisp aptly calls "'Butch Cassidy and the Sundance Kid' with a sex change") the handsome stud puppy Brad Pitt gets a chance to stick it to Geena Davis in a Texas motel room. Trouble is, explains the star, "They spend so much time beforehand doing things like covering up the zits on your ass that during the actual scene, you're numb. It's over before you know it. All I remember is feeling very good driving home that night."

Well, so did we, Brad, after seeing you in that terrific little movie. And so did some girls, whom we overheard dishing: "Oh, oh, this is that cute, outlaw, hitchhiker seducer-boy from 'Thelma and Louise.' If he hadn't stolen all their money he'd be perfect."

Another: "I'm too young to get into movies like that. But I must admit he looks almost cuddly enough to be in my 'Non-Threatening Boys' magazine."

Commented David Denby: "A slender young drifter who presents himself as 'a student,' he is sly and exquisitely polite, demure even though he prances like a show horse. He's obviously no student, but Thelma, goosey as a teenager, finds him irresistible. What follows is one of the rare sex scenes that manage to be funny and truly erotic at the same time. There's one glamorized shot of Brad Pitt's torso that suggests a commercial for sex..."

(Can't you just see it, "Brad Pitt for Sex." Yum yum.)

Critic Holly Millea says she's "Mad for Brad:" "Lean, all legs and lips and liquid movement." And he's talented. As Brad's "Louise" director Lou Di Giaimo says, "There are stars that aren't great actors. But when I met Brad, I thought, 'He's going to be a star and he can act.' His career is going to be capital B-I-G." He got the part when Billy Baldwin backed out to appear in "Backdraft."

Big or not so big, the star protests: "Oh, I'm a pencil neck. I'm no Schwarzenegger." No, but as Melina Gerosa notes, "Pitt's washboard stomach, smoldering stare, and all-around boyish allure have the hype types predictably touting him as the next James Dean." But the 27-year-old Oklahoma-born, Missouri-bred actor has heard enough of the comparison: "There's this thing about every young new guy getting compared to James Dean. I've read it a million times, even about Michael J. Fox." He claims he never even thought about acting when he came to Holywood. He was going to further his education in graphic design. "Things open up for you," he says. Indeed. Now he's the toast of London with his ads for Levi's plastered all over town and in commercials in heavy rotation on the BBC (unfortunately, they won't be shown in the U.S.A.) and, with several movies coming out, the single actor is beginning to feel the weight of celebrity. He lives alone in West Hollywood and tries to keep a low profile. "My buddies kind of abuse me because I don't leave the house much. You know, when you reach a point where you just have fun in a box by yourself?"

(Okay, Brad baby, if you say so.)

He goes on, "If people are going to be interested in what's popping out of your mouth when it moves, you oughta have something going for you. You've got to be responsible. Sometimes it makes me want to move up into the mountains."

(Hey, Brad, if you get lonely up in those mountains, here's my number...oh, and, please, call collect. You're worth it.)

Rupert Everett

"Another Country." What a perfect title for a perfect film to star Rupert Everett. After meeting young blond Cary Elwes at boarding school and having a delicate, beautifully filmed affair, his character turns into a famous spy.

Since that breakthrough which heartened us boywatchers, his screen appearances have been few but choice. In "Dance With a Stranger" the older woman that loves him ends up killing him and, in "The Comfort of Strangers," a tale of sexual self-destruction, he spends much of the time in the nude. (He says he worked out with a German fellow and it showed.) For gays, it was a fascinating exercise. Early in the film, an older man takes Everett and his female lover to a gay bar in Venice for a drink. It becomes clear that the older man is obsessed with the younger one. The bar scene clearly foreshadows the plot. "This is the real Venice," the woman (played by Natasha Richardson) comments.

We also discover Everett is just becoming aware of his own homosexual desires. At one point, he asks Natasha, "What does it feel like, to be the woman?" Often criticized about his treatment of homosexuality in earlier works ("American Gigolo" for one) director Paul Schrader says, "I've been accused of seeing homosexuality as dangerous. The truth is, you should take off the 'homo' part. I think all sexuality is dangerous. I guess it comes from my background (Midwestern Calvinist). There's an element of aggression and fear to sexual relations that no amount of liberations is going to dispel. And when you step out of traditional roles, the danger has to go up. It's one thing for a bisexual man to be rejected by a woman. It's another to be rejected by a man. With a man, it's almost like being rejected twice. First I get ejected for coming out, then I get rejected by the person I came out to." In the film, it's the stolidly spoiled Everett who is meant to be the film's object of beauty. As Bob Satuloff said, "Turning heads in trattorias, inspiring secret admirers, all but stopping traffic on the Grand Canal." Satuloff shrugged the film off as "mock Bertolucci-strenuously atmospheric and lushly overscored." Perhaps, but then it does have Everett, a sight we can't get enough of.

"Everett is properly arrogant and sardonic without being fey," says Rex Reed, who, let's face it, knows fey. "His shady elegance and petulant lips translate into a barely contained rebelliousness that echoes early Brando or Dean," raves critic Jane Goodman. The star retorts, "Not early Dean. Maybe later Dean."

As reported by Brandon Judell, Rupert just doesn't know how to turn off the heat: "Think of Olivier in 'Wuthering Heights' and you'd still have to throw a few Duraflame logs to attain the right intensity."

The actor lives in France in the wintertime when it's completely desolate. "I've become a loner," he says. "I'm not quite sure how. It's one of those things that suddenly creeps up on you, then you're just one and there's nothing you can do about it."

But occasionally he will venture out to participate in some show biz hoopla, such as the premiere of Madonna's "Truth or Dare" at Cannes, where the material girl's fantasy of kissing a woman while others watch took an interesting spin when she dared Seymour Stein (Sire Records president) to French-kiss Rupert for fifteen seconds. A voyeur reported: "The next thing we knew, Stein had a recording contract." At the same party, Madonna asked Roman Polanski who his first sexual experience was with and he said, "A boy."

One wonders how Rupert would have answered that question.

Robert Downey Jr.

"In 'Less Than Zero' I played a guy who's bisexual," Robert Downey Jr. says about his riskiest role, "and I do a scene with my underwear down and my head between some guy's legs. If I was convincing - and I think I was - it was because I was in the moment. I was paying attention. I was also thinking that there's nothing worse than seeing an actor not commit to something that's uncomfortable."

Speaking of being uncomfortable, the 26-year-old actor says the most regrettable thing he's ever done occurred when he was in Amsterdam. "I went to the red-light district and I was really, really perturbed by what I saw. I thought it was going to be like little treasures from Helsinki, but, in fact, it was vile. Strange even to the strange. I went into a bookstore and I opened book. I should have known. It was like 'Kindersex' and 'Habensex.' Child sex, dark sex. And then I saw this animal thing and the minute I opened it, I thought, Oh, fuck, it's too late. I've alreay seen it; now it's logged in there forever: 'Hundsex.' Dog sex. I can see it right now. There it is, that jazzed-up chick right on this Rottweiler's schnitzel!"

Again in 1991, in the screwy comedy "Too Much Sun," Robert plays a dissolute young hustler, this time one who tries to satisfy two gay giblings desperate to produce a child in order to inherit their father's fortune, directed by his father, Robert Sr. (of "Putney Swope" fame). Critic David Ehrenstein comments: "It is the work of someone who thinks being gay or lesbian is in and of itself some sort of joke." Bob Satuloff thought that Downey Jr. was the only actor in the film to "give off any degree of steam by abandoning his father's script completely. "What he does has little to do with the movie he's in but at least it's amusing."

During a production meeting, Downey confronted one of the producers by asking: "'Are you gay? Do you like the idea of another man's hand on your penis? Can you accept the fact that everyone is bisexual?' And they go, 'Oh! Oh!' Every six minutes the table would like blow up!" Robert wanted to pattern his performance after Montgomery Clift but the producers thought more along the lines of James Dean. "Well," Downey laughed, "that was okay because Dean was kind of a speedy bisexual."

"I think a lot of it is sexual. I don't have any hangups about 'gay stuff.' It's a very homophobic business. I know gay people in positions of power. A: everybody knows. B: it shouldn't matter. They should tell them, 'You're already where you want to be, it's not going to affect you one way or another.'

"As for myself, I think 'heterosexuality' and 'homosexuality' are overspecifications. A lot of my peer group think I'm an eccentric bisexual, like I may even have an ammonia-filled tentacle or something somewhere on my body. That's ok. Being relaxed about sexuality is something you're born with. It's just part of your personality before you show up." If he's ever been with a guy sexually, he won't say. "If I had, I wouldn't want to say because I wouldn't want a studio head to think that I was less capable of portraying someone who needed to be very masculine or that I sucked dick for beer money."

(Hey, handsome, what would you do for champagne money?)

Teen Heartthrobs

Of the seven ages of man, adolescence may be the most tumultuous. It's also the most boring, at least to the outsider. Teenagers are feeling their way to adulthood, resisting mightily traditional values. They are a pain in the ass: alienated from their parents, tortured in various predictable ways, full of high but untested ideals, and, most importantly of all it seems, obsessed with getting it on.

And for Hollywood, all this makes for superb fodder for the movies and TV. For writers and directors, it gives them a chance to replay their childhood and give themselves better scores this time around.

And each year we see a bumper crop of new kids on the block, ready to fuel these fantasies. Where do they come from, these dazzlers? Just lucky? No, for most of them they hit it big only after years of hard work, and then only because they got just the right role in a hit movie or a hit TV show.

But to become an idol of gaymales takes a bit of doing because he's got to show us a bit of himself, make himself sensitive to us, vulnerable, yet wise in the ways of the world. We wait, patiently, to see what happens, forever clinging to the hope that in the next movie perhaps the star will take all his clothes off and be everything we pray he is.

Jason Priestley

A star overnight perhaps, but an actor of many years standing, sexy Jason Priestley got into showbiz as a child in his native Canada, appearing in dog food and Tonka toy commercials. But the drive to appear was all his; his mother is about as far from a stage mom as one could get and she used to charge Jason to drive him to auditions. "Why do I have to pay?" he'd ask her. And she would respond, "Well, if I didn't have to drive you, you'd have to take a cab and you'd have to pay the cab driver."

Arriving in California, he didn't work for a year, spending the money he had saved in Canada at an incredible rate and soon he had no money but he had lots of fun. "My friend and I had this car, a '68 Cadillac. We used to drive it around. The car was huge. We called it the Homesmobile. Then we lived in this little North Hollywood apartment. It was wild. I look back on it now and it was the most fun I ever had in my life."

(Makes you wish you'd been there, with all that room in the backseat to play around in.)

"I went back to Vancouver and then got offered a film role in Hollywood so I came back and now here I am."

Here he is indeed. As Brandon on "Beverly Hills 90210," a twin who is uprooted from his Minnesota home when his family moves to the posh L.A. suburb, he plays a character whose new classmates accept him almost immediately but because his values are different from his peers, problems arise.

His acting seems effortless, honed over years of appearing before the camera as a model and in the short-lived series "Sister Kate" and Disney Channel specials.

But Jason's ultimate goal is to direct. "It's just another form of expression. What I do is very visual but as a director you go to another level of physical expression. You use the camera as a tool of expression."

Hey, Jason, pretty Jason, we can think of some other nifty tools of expression...

Billy Warlock

"He's back!" Much to the delight of the fans of Billy Warlock, he returned to the daytime soaper, "Days of Our Lives," as Frankie Donner. The adorable hazel-eyed urchin left the show in 1989 to co-star in the "Baywatch" series on NBC, which was subsequently cancelled. Upon his return, Billy was promptly voted favorite male soap star by *Teen Beat* magazine readers.

Young Billy's fame has come after many years of hard work. He was featured on as Flip on "Happy Days" and was a stunt man for Mork on "Mork & Mindy," once rolling down a steep hill on roller stakes, up an incline, and off a 50-foot cliff. No wimp, this cutie.

As one fan put it, "There's just something about him that makes him simply irresistible. Maybe it's his innocent-looking face or those eyes or his winsome smile. Or maybe it's all those things and more!" We can dream can't we...about the "more?"

Corey Haim

Over the years, I've become obsessed with the 5' 4", 113#, blond, blue-eyed bundle of fun named Corey Haim. And I'm not alone.

I first fell head over heels in lust for the tyke in 1986's "Lucas," which has as one of its many delights a realistic shower sequence at a high school gym. Then came the stylish vampire comedy "Lost Boys" in which the cutie takes a very sexy bath.

By 1989, Corey was getting rave reviews for his fine thesping. About "Dream a Little Dream," one reviewer raved: "Goofy Corey Haim lends his light and silly charm to provide the few laughs in this film."

And, by then, Corey had became a darling of the teenyboppers. Haimster mania set in. There was even a calendar featuring scenes of the adorable lad in scenes from the horrible horror movie "The Watchers."

But suddenly it seemed Corey was overcome by it all; he started hanging out in Hollywood's infamous fast lane. The reports were discouraging. Like me, Larry Clark, photographer and creator of the best-selling books "Tulsa" and "Teenage Lust," had become enamored of the sexy little star and fretted about his survival. Larry says: "He is this beautiful little kid, this actor kid, and then he got into drugs, and it's so weird to see in the magazine photographs of what happened to him in just a few months. But then he came back and got a 900 number.

"I was curious so I called and he went into this incredible rap about how he was all fucked up on cocaine. He was saying things like 'You just wouldn't believe how everyone in L.A. does cocaine and I was doing so much cocaine I got down to about ninety pounds and my mother put me in rehab.' He must have just got out because he sounded like a reformed drunk: 'I'd rather cut off my arm and throw it out on the expressway than ever do coke again.' He was freaking out. And then I read some articles about it. Now he's probably trying to forget he ever said those things, trying to rehabilitate his image."

Later in the year, Corey appeared in his own video,"Me, Myself and I." His publicist was saying the star wanted to clear **the air, to** counter rumors that had been flying about him: "We did it to let people know what's really happening in my life. I just wanted people not to still have the wrong impression of me after everything that went down. Things are back to normal now." The 45-minute video includes Corey talking about his life, what it was like before he became an actor, scenes of him playing hockey and baseball (and the one we loved, floating on a raft in a swimming pool), driving his new sports car and his thoughts on the perfect date. Corey's sage advice: "Take the hurdles in life that come to you. Everybody has lots obstacles to overcome. Just go through them, be patient and everything will happen."

So great was Corey's popularity with girls, even while he was taking the cure, he was voted "Male Movie Star of the Year" by *Teen Beat* readers. When he got out of rehab he appeared in *Teen Beat's* first video format magazine, talking about the movies and taking questions from an audience of screaming young girls. He handled it well although he appeared to be more "out-of-it" than "with-it."

And he was back in the fast lane again, hanging out with other stud puppies such as Josh Evans, the handsome young son of producer Robert Evans, and Balthazar Getty at Hollywood's fashionable Sunset Social Club, presumably drinking Perrier.

In 20-year-old Corey's "comeback" film, CineTel Films' "Fast Getaway," he played the 16-year-old son of a bank robber. After testing poorly with preview audiences in 1991, the film went directly to video stores, where his gay fans could rent it and enjoy his scenes in tight jeans and drag in the privacy of their own homes.

Then came "Dream Machine," which also went directly to video. *Entertainment Weekly* commented: "Reformed party animal Haim plays a clean-up piano tuner who inherits a Porsche with a corpse in the trunk and is pursued by a killer. If this is meant to be a teen action comedy, just where are the laughs?" Next Corey was on rollerskates for "Prayer of the Rollerboys," still billed over-the-title and co-starring with Patricia Arquette. This bomb also went directly to video.

Now, if it'd only have been called "Prayer of the Gayboys..."

Sex in Art

The New Artists: "We Think a Lot About Penises"

The current renaissance of lesbian and gay representation in art is an acknowledgement by galleries and academia, if not museums, that these artists have something important to say. But this coalescence has taken centuries of exposure to occur and, as reported by noted art critic David Hirsh, the emergence of "this wild beast from the 'margins' of society" is due to an outpouring of creativity borne on death and assault as much as celebration of sexuality and individuality.

One of the key examples of this renaissance was an exhibit in New York, "Out and Exposed," in which 21 artists were represented, most of whom were consciously reaching for universal response, as did past generations of artists who were lesbian or gay.

"The point," Hirsh maintains, "is that their experience as homosexuals allows them to address the human condition with just as much authority and insight as the experience of others. The new generation, however, was weaned on the explosions of AIDS, censorship, and feminist inquiry."

In the early '80s, clubs were the main outlet available to gay artists to exhibit their works. But now that galleries are accepting gay work, they have replaced the clubs as a meeting ground for artists and what we are seeing is an ambition and depth of talent that is suprising many in the mainstream art world.

One of the most talented gay artists is George Towne, who paints and draws realistic male figures, sometimes nude, figures that have become more and more isolated over the years. "Yet," Hirsh says, "the painting remains sensual and loving in its investigation of masculinity. The artist says, "It's a political agenda to be out to everyone I know. The macho image is interesting to me. I admire the monumental quality of Atilla Lukacs's work, as well as Anselim Kiefer and Rainer Fetting. In my next series, I'll try to express the spirit that one would get at an AIDS demonstration."

Robert Clarke draws blatantly sexual figures, as exhibited in his

MFA Graduate Show. Often concentrating on fantasies of power (like phallic power), he is "unconcerned with realistic settings" and there can be a childlike rendering in his images. He explains: "Homosexuality became an important reason for me to make things in the summer of 1988. Being called a 'gay artist' used to bother me, but now I see it as a strength. It represents a commitment to a subject matter. My work is autobiographical in that I try to be honest about what turns me on; it's almost adolescent masturbatory fantasies. I want to reach large groups of people."

Childlike figurations are also painted by W. H. Myers, sometimes sexual, sometimes humorous, sometimes in a hospital setting, always focusing on expressive gay issues. Even when dealing with sexualized male forms, Mark Chamberlain reaches for spiritual insight. He says, "I'm interested in narratives which relate to a cogent moment. My photographs document full experience, things that are personal about social realms, like the Gay Pride Parade and Wigstock. I use male icons from television and magazines, responding to media culture. It's directly autobiographical, working through to a resolution."

Alex Heimberg's drawings refer to early medieval art, Expressionist woodprints, and urban psychedelic forms. He colors his art with construction paper and markers, yet is perhaps most involved with Xerox duplications of these pieces. He arouses sexual feelings by having erect penises become blunt icons. Cocks also figured prominently in Joseh A. Kaminiski's show "Dick & Me." His photographs and drawings of the phallus garnered the biggest crowds of the year at the New York co-op gallery of which he is a member.

Matthew Weinstein's vibrant paintings contain basic shapes suggest Pop emblems which, Hirsh says, "vibrate in an abstract evocation of desire." The ideas in a current series of paintings were suggested by Bruno Bettelheim's 1959 essay, "Joey, A Mechanical Boy." Using the idea of the fragmented and isolated body, positioning circles or balls in various configurations of sensual attraction, coexistence or repulsion, the artist's abstraction encourages us to "consider our most conflicted relationship, which is between our bodies and ourselves." In his series, he attempted to simulate the experience of embarrassment when you look at someone's body too much. "I think that painting can embarrass us your own body. In the Renaissance, the imagery may have been religious but it was about flesh rendering flesh and seducing through that. My painting is more about experience than meaning. I want to tap that side of painting that is illusion and seduction."

One of the leading galleries in New York exhibiting gay work is Wessel O'Connor, run by John Wessel and Bill O'Connor. At 580 Broadway, a mainline art address in Manhattan, they put on a show simply titled "Queer." "It is a word that provokes no small amount of controversy in the gay communty these days," explains critic Douglas Turnbaugh, "but it was the word of choice for the 64 gay and lesbian artists who crowded the gallery walls with a diverse representation of work from painting to conceptual art." But Wessell complains: "The straight press is screwing us. We've had only one real *New York Times* review in four years, and I can't name a sympathetic art magazine. We have our good friends in the press but it's 'no names, please.' And we have our gay brothers in every single museum but they are afraid of opening confrontational art. How many gay shows have you seen in the three major New York museums? Yet all the major curators are gay."

During the year Wessell featured the work of the popular Bruce of Los Angeles, a master of the so-called "Southern California nude" in the '50s and '60s. "Today," Wessel says, "nobody remembers that in his time he was harassed constantly, his prints confiscated and destroyed by the postal authorities."

John Lindell had three simultaneous exhibits which highlighted the growth of a formal and poetic vocabulary rooted in gay sex. The artist went so far as to provide an explanatory kit for the representations of totally sensualized male bodies surrounding the Social Structures. Symbols for erogenous body parts -the anus, nipple, lips, glans, etc. - are drawn onto the walls to form several figures. Hirsh says: "The room becomes a surreal congregation of men engrossed in pleasant fantasies." He goes on to explain: "For centuries artists have sought expansive codes or symbols for personal forbidden desires. Inverting this tradition, Lindell uses a large array of materials and current formal techniques to expose his sources. Yet this honesty does not negate the wish to affect a diverse audience; rather, it affirms that personal works by artists who are gay have equal access to human emotions. Lindell is among those energetic formalists intent on personalizing, humanizing or otherwise 'corrputing' the aesthetics of purity." The artist himself said: "I want to depict sex acts, the acts I know, between men, in the most neutralized way possible so that people can think with their own images. I want to keep the discussion of sex as dry as possible so that one is forced back into one's own memory. Camp draws too much attention to itself. My symbols can become a language because they're a realm we accept as neutral. It goes back to an interest in relying on memory. Think of how much memory and daydreaming is devoted to sex and romance; it's a huge amount of one's day. So it seems like a natural topic."

That "natural topic" is, in the words of artist Nowell Nesbitt, "the hardest thing to sell. On the Richter scale, male nude drawings have a shock value around 10 - just about the hardest thing to show and sell." His own art, he says, are portraits of the body. "The reason I do so many frontal nudes is that it's lovely to have a conversation while the model is posing. I don't make special requests or ask the model to take any particular pose. At the first meeting, the model will take different positions in slow motion. I take Polaroids, which I give to the model, when I see something that's interesting to me. I have kind of a clinical attitude. We mutually agree on the final poose. You wouldn't believe the kinds of fantasies which some models themselves have."

In search of models to show the different ways sex continues within the AIDS crisis, Brian Weil went to Thailand because it's known as the sex capital of the world. "The tourist industry is based on the sex trade," the artist explains. "The price of sex and drugs is related to the spread of AIDS. In the expensive clubs, the boys get $40 and have a low diseaase rate. They have maybe one or two clients a week. As it gets cheaper, the boys have more clients and the disease rate goes up. I met youths near the train station that pick up farmers and people coming into the city from the country-side and they were charging 40 to 75 cents." The reason his photographs are distorted and grainy is because they never deal with the destruction of the body. "It releases the photographs from the architecture of the disease," he says, "which is really just the surface of it. You can deal metaphorically with the political, social, and moral issues."

Humanity, maybe? That's what Danny Garcia, an artist who moved from L.A. to New York, says: "My art is about society's idea of perversion. They may call it perverse but it's what they do at home behind closed doors." Such activities, as subjects, have included bestiality, pedophilia, and violent sex acts. One of his paintings was removed from a gallery in L.A. when patrons complained. On an 18' x 12' canvas, he depicted five kids having an orgy on a window sill while below a woman is giving birth and all the while a dark angel is watching. "I'm trying to depict society's oppression," the artist states. "My latest painting is based on an actual story I saw on the news. It was about this kid in the ghetto who killed himself because he thought his younger brothers and sisters would have more to eat if he was gone. The painting, called 'I Am Death In Love With Death,' shows an angel nailed to a wall." The artist signs his paintings "Leer Von Gar." The "Leer" is his gaze upon society, the "Von" is his tribute to his German Expressionism influence, and "Gar" is the first three letter of his last name. The artist first realized he was gay when he was eleven. "I was even younger when I first had sex with other kids. I told my parents I was gay when I was sixteen. They were totally accepting. As it turns out, I have an older brother who is gay too. We came out at about the same time, though I knew about him before then. I snooped around his room and found his porn magazines."

Lesbians, too, often find artistic inspiration in the power of the phallus. Daphne Fitzpatrick uses male midsections for examination, pleasure and humor. "I started drawing penises because they're mysterious to me; it's relieved a lot of anxiety. The drawings came out of life size photographs of naked men I did. I'm investigating something I don't know about."

"With the mainstream cultural doors opening," Hirsh concludes, "the promise of rich discoveries of feeling and love will tempt exploration by the most insightful artists." As Wessel says, "Our shows are going to continue to be confrontational and provocative. We think a lot about pensises, but we do think about other things too."

Christopher Ciccone

The Wessel O'Connor Gallery scored a coup during the year by exhibiting the works of Madonna's brother Christopher. "There's no getting away from the fact that she is my sister," says the 30-year-old artist. "I came to New York eight years ago and realized I could paint. And then my sister got famous and she needed somebody to do certain things for her, like design sets and houses, and that gave me the opportunities to do things in which I have no training. Her position gave me an opportunity and I made the best of it."

Indeed. Wessel says: "He's not an unknown person. He can't stop being his sister's brother. But it helps that she doesn't use her last name. Many collectors and colleagues don't know and wouldn't care." O'Connor adds: "He does good painting. He's a serious artist. He's someone in for the long run."

Madonna says: "He's searching for the truth. His work is full of symbolism and metaphor." When the material girl outed him, little brother said: "If only my sister would stay out of my life, everything would be fine. If I were more like her, I would have made use of that opportunity. But since I'm not, either the effect has been limited or I just don't realize it. People don't like to feel their lives are out of control or that they can't control their own destinies. Being gay is neither the place I begin from nor the place I end at. I don't paint gay paintings or homoerotic imagery. The thing that separates me from the rest of the world is the way I think, not the way I have sex. Everyone is drawn to one's sexuality but it's not that important."

One of his paintings, "Figurate," contains a headless, limbless male with no genitalia because, says he, it would be a distraction from seeing the form. "I'm not interested in the emotion there."

Wessel says Chris' paintings are "like a dream he had that he's trying to paint before it fades away. Yes, I think they're homoerotic. I also find the truncated bodies recall the epidemic. These paintings are a very gentle document on harsh times."

Bruce Weber: "Sexual Rhythms"

"The art establishment," critic Brian Morgante says, "ever suspicious of fashion photographers, has never embraced Bruce Weber. There is also discomfort with the sexual rhythms of Weber's work. Ironically, no commercial photographer has ever had the exposure and free rein that Weber has had in his multi-page advertisements for Calvin Klein and Ralph Lauren. His daydreams posit homosex as a full Platonic ideal, not as the expression of an injured psyche. The censure comes from heterosexuals feeling left out or deprived, quite a turnaround."

During 1991, Weber had his first solo show in L.A. and demonstrated "a spectacular grasp of composition." He is so accomplished he can use nudes to express a full range of values and ideas. "His early classicism has given way to a mature style that enables him to allow more ambiguity into the pictures."

Also during the year, two books were published which celebrated this great talent. The first, "Bruce Weber," was dedicated to his sister, who took him to his first rock concert and left him there, to find his own way home. "The photoghraphs are very cool and they've got a lot of that Weber warmth," applauded *Interview*. "Who and what are in it? John Lee Hooker's looking good with a feather in his hat. Naomi Campbell's got Mike Tyson on the ground, pinned, and the King, Don King, is cheering them on. Siegfried and Roy are doing up some magic cutting someone in half, we swear. And Robert Mitchum's so charming you could flip. Great models. And Paris is Paris like it should be: watery, gray, romantic. And there's plenty more. You can feel Weber's eyes landing on subjects that mean something to him, such as Eduard Boubat, that distinguished photographer most people have forgotten about by now. On top of all this, along with a piece by William Burroughs, Weber has given us something priceless: truth, in the form of an essay that describes growing up in Greensburg, Pennsylvania, and his life with his parents, who also appear among the images."

The images in Bruce's second big book of the year, "Bear Pond," delighted gaymale audiences. It is a delicious, hardbound but not hardcore, recording of a fun-filled weekend with some beautiful men. Weber is donating the proceeds from this best-seller to benefit AIDS research.

Robert Indiana

"Love is central to my life," Robert Clarke, known to the art world as Robert Indiana, says. Indeed. He apotheosized the sixties when he designed his "Love" sign for a Museum of Modern Art Christmas card and eventually it ended up on 330 million stamps. More than 20 years later, both "Love" and its creator have fallen on hard times.

First about the symbol: The stacked-letter design with the cat's eye 0: the creator never copyrighted it so, despite his own endless stream of variations in paintings, prints, and sculptures, there were millions of unauthorized uses, from bumper stickers to wastepaper baskets for which he received nary a penny. "The only thing it wasn't on was toilet paper," the artist jokes, "and I was surprised about that."

Now, in sexuality's darkest hour, the artist is feeling a backlash. Love, so central to his life, has become his undoing. On a quiet day in August 1990, the law came to Clarke's home in Maine, on the little island of Vinalhaven (population 1,200), search warrant in hand. Inside the artist's three-story Victorian refuge, a former Odd Fellows lodge decked out with curios and memorabilia, the law conducted a search. By nightfall, they had handcuffed the artist and were transferring him to the mainland aboard a Coast Guard boat. It seems nine of Indiana's latest love-inspired drawings were explicit studies of male genitalia. The charges made against him were: two criminal complaints of engaging a prostitute and one of patronizing the prostitution of a minor.

In the request for the search warrant, it was revealed that two men, ages nineteen and twenty-one, had posed for the artist in the nude for fees ranging from $20 to $200. Along with their posing, they also engaged in sex acts. One of the men said that this sordid behavior had been going on for years, ever since he was an adolescent. One young man knew it was wrong but said he was "doing it for the money." The whole thing started when Jason Marriner, one of the young men who posed nude, stole checks from the artist and others and went to the cops to bargain for a slap on the wrist.

Further investigation revealed the young man had forged over $7,000 in checks. Indiana claims he would never have filed charges but, by then, the damage was done. Another model, John MacDonald, corroborated Marriner's story about being paid to pose and for sex. All this proved very titillating to the residents of the tiny island. After all, openly gay Clarke's loud arguments with his lovers over the years had been the talk of the town.

The writer Paul Taylor comments: "Ever since the nation entered the age of AIDS, America's moralist minority has been on a witch-hunt and the name of Robert Indiana, whether he likes it or not, is closely identified with the free-love movement. His being charged with paying for sex suggests that free love has become very expensive indeed."

The three-man artists' co-op called General Idea bastardized the Love symbol to make "AIDS," and, as Love did, the revision idea speaks volumes about the world we live in. It has become a tragic distortion of the face of Love.

But Indiana doesn't mind. "It's what I would have one myself because the association of love with AIDS is inevitable, one of the ironic twists of coincidence. But I wouldn't have made it as grotesque as theirs. Their 'D' is grotesque."

It seems appropriate that the symbol become recognized as a sign of the times for programs that are springing up to promote artistic collaboration between artists and persons with AIDS. These exhibitions are in line with the intention of AIDS Artreach to become an ongoing project instead of one big show and to make AIDS a public issue. AIDS has become an issue for artists because so many are dying of it every year. It provides a possibility of expression for those with the disease and the stigmatisation of the HIV-infected person can be understood as a metaphor for the stigmatisation of the artist in our society.

If anyone knows about stigmatisation of the artist, it's Robert Indiana. When he was part of the New York art scene, moving there in 1954 from Indiana, the artist was known mostly as stand-offish, a cold fish, perhaps arising from his lifelong history as an outsider. Taylor explains: "Although there were divisions among the little band of artists in those days they were all unified in isolation from the swaggering abstract expressionist heroes of Greenwich Village by their softer, more sophisticated sensibilities and from the uptown art scene by their indigence...Indiana would often attend art openings uptown because he needed to eat. In addition to their isolation, the hidden homosexuality of the subculture's prime movers prompted cliquish behavior - secrecy and ambiguity on the one hand, exaggerated conformity on the other. Like Whitman, who wrote, 'I dare not tell it in words, not even in these songs,' more than one artist on the waterfront used code words and symbols to stand in for forbidden subject matter. By depicting the inside of the proverbial Closet, their art epitomized the conflicted gay sensibility of the day."

In recent years the artist has been enjoying some of the recognition that had eluded him for so long. This print retrospective (from 1951 to the present, and including two new versions of "Love, 1991") was a smashing success. On the resale market, his works are fetching respectable prices. Two years ago, Taylor reports, a "Love" painting went for almost $145,000 at auction in France and "One Indiana Square" (commissioned in 1970 by the Indiana National Bank in Indianapolis for $10,000) is on the market for a six-figure amount.

Indiana's new work may well be inspired by his legal problems. In later years, Indiana revealed that the tilted "O" in "Love" was an erection and he had an obsession with the phallus. That obsession, you could safely say, became the root of all evil for Robert Indiana.

Sex in Literature

"One thing Americans have in excess is idle time," Russell Baker says, "but they hate to admit it." The astonishing statistics on how many hours the typical person now spends watching TV seem to belie the fact that most people assure us there simply aren't enough hours in the day. "This is a very romantic way to look at ourselves," Baker observes. "It's like clapping yourself on the back for leading such a full, rich and vigorous life.

"But people who trade in the printed word are getting positively morose about the suspicion that Americans are reading less than they used to. Whether the suspicion is justifiable is hard to say, but what's interesting here is the apparent determination of book people to talk themselves into a mental depression. 'Print's musty and old-fashioned,' they fear.

"But it isn't the lack of time that keeps people from reading. It's the lack of interest in the subjects. When the subject interests them, they'll buy books by the mile."

Indeed. Consider the year's bumper crop of books if not about sex, with at least a high sexual quotient. While they might not sell in Peoria, they do elsewhere. "While an unlettered society does not rush out to buy books that question the American dream," says Michael O'Louglin, "disenfranchised readers are hungry for books that reflect their existence. This is something most independent publishers have known for a long time, something the mainstream publishing houses are now catching onto. There is a sizable number of readers who relish living on the edge of respectable society - true adventurers and 'hip' dillettantes in search of a trend, a fresh voice, a new angle."

Critic Bob Satuloff says, "This has proven to be something of a banner year for gay novels. With works of such superior quality and storytelling skill as Neil Bartlett's 'Ready to Catch Him Should He Fall,' Peter McGehee's 'Boys Like Us,' Joe Keenan's 'Putting on the Ritz,' and Paul Monette's 'Halfway Home,' leading a large and impressive array of books, gay writers are demonstrating not only a high degree of eloquence, vitality, and much-needed humor, as well as burgeoning and necessary commerciality, but are expanding the borders of the popular concept of gay writing. No longer confined to coming out sagas or chronicles of oppression by a brutally insensitive straight world, gay-identified novels can now have as their subject matter virtually anything the traffic will bear."

Dennis Cooper

Rebel writer Dennis Cooper's books have all dealt graphically with sexual obsession and violence and it's amazing they get published by a mainstream publisher but they do. And while favorably reviewed in mainstream publications, his newest adventure, "Frisk," was not well received by several key gay columnists. A critic for *The Bay Area Reporter* thought it was a "punishing retread of a nauseating topic from an author who is creatively bankrupt." At one reading, the author was even confronted by a male member of the Hookers' United Liberation Army, pushing a pamphlet in his face with the words "Dennis Cooper Must Die!" scrawled across it. Said the boy, "If I try to talk, I'll get too angry, but as a male hustler, I want you to know what you're exploiting and profiting off of."

Profiting indeed. The best-selling hardcover "Frisk" deals with a man's obsession with torturing and killing male sex objects, a theme that Cooper has mined extensively. "But it's not my whole sensibility," he claimed in an interview with Adam Block. "I take reponsibility for (the narrator's) thoughts and actions because I could imagine myself doing them. But I'm not exactly like the character. I'm not completely obsessed. I have a life. See, I want to understand these interests that I've had since I was a kid. The farthest I can trace it back is to reading de Sade's '120 Days of Sodom' at 15. I remember being absolutely amazed, horrified, and turned on. It was only later that I realized that it was fiction. I had thought there might be a real world like the one de Sade described, where people explored each other as sources of information about life or desire. Then I realized that you don't really have a right to use people like that.

"If I do have a message it's that I'm interested in this stuff and trying to present it in a way that allows the readers to explore it too. Much of the criticism has been about the subject matter and the way

I've treated it rather than my writing. I think critics expect books to provide answers. But my intent is to do something else; I want to provoke an examination in the reader of these forbidden things. Everybody expects when you're supposed to come to some kind of enlightenment, and there is none. There is no answer to things as complicated as violence or sex. My book isn't superficial or exploitative, but there are people who think that if you write about this stuff without explicitly rejecting it or interpreting it as the result of child abuse, then you're not dealing with it in a serious way. That's a failing of theirs.

"I can't control people's interests. We'd never write about anything horrifying if we thought that every time someone picked up a book, they'd want to do what they read about. I mean, there might be a lot of people who pick up a book by David Leavitt, read it and decide to become boring yuppies. That horrifies me. Leavitt's work is banal. He is not a good writer. Real grade-school John Cheever. I'm sorry but then I'm uninterested in almost all mainstream gay writers. I like experimental fiction. Mainstream gay culture irritates me. I used to be romantic and think that queers were privileged by being outsiders. I hoped they would understand that and create some alternatives - fight the system, not buy into it. I'd like to see the whole thing blown up. I'm an anarchist. Still, I think people should be able to have child-subsitute pets and computers, go to bars every night, drink booze and listen to boring records."

The incident with the hustler angers him. "The last thing I want to do is to have those kids think I'm exploiting them. They seem to think that I'm proposing the actions in 'Frisk' as acceptable. But actually the opposite is true. These kids are in a lot of pain. So are they expected to read my books in a sophisticated way? No. The whole issue is complicated. I'm walking a fine line in the book. I'm presenting a dangerous sensibility without saying directly, This is bad.

"I'm just trying to confront people with certain transgressive urges that are usually repressed and make them examine themselves for signs of those urges. I could never claim to be as brave as those kids, and I'm really glad I got a chance to talk with them. It made me think a lot about what art can do - the difference between making people confront their ideas alone with a book and devoting actual time to helping real kids. I've always felt that I ought to do more, but I have a hard time dealing with that stuff in real life."

Colin McPhee

One book authored by the largely forgotten composer Colin McPhee and one book written about him appeared during 1991, both to great acclaim. The reissue of McPhee's own book, "A House in Bali," was termed by one New York reviewer as "a minor literary masterpiece." No critic recognized it as such or even acknowledged its presence when it was published in 1946, but today it is widely admired for its observations of cultures in conflict and a sophisticated but unaffected narrative style.

"Bali" is concerned with the composer's life on the island during the 1930s and does not hint at the existence of his wife, Jane, who supported him through the period. What it does discuss is his relationships with the young male dancers, musicians and houseboys who are the principals in his cast of characters, and, given the publishing restrictions of the time, could not have been more explicit.

In Carol J. Oja's biography of the composer, "Composer in Two Worlds," she attributes the breakup of their marriage in 1938 to her increasing humiliation from Colin's openly flaunted homosexuality or rather, pederasty, since the reference is probably to Sampih, his adopted pre-teen-age boy. McPhee himself cites the same cause in a letter to his friend Sidney Cowell, the wife of Henry Cowell, a man who spent four years in San Quentin for the same "crime" before being proven innocent.

Jane McPhee was fully aware of her husband's sexual proclivities from the beginning of their relationship, as well as her own inclinations toward women. Indeed, she had been involved in the late 1930s in a witchhunt when 34 young female dancers were interrogated regarding her sexual behavior.

Both McPhees were attracted to the exotic. McPhee himself once wrote, "The moment I am among Negroes I feel strangely at peace and happy. I wish I'd lived in Harlem." Most of his friends were similarly inclined. He writes of the time a visiting regent was being waited on by one of his handsome young retainers. The regent's gaze settled on the boy, after which "his eyes met mine in a glance of insolent penetration."

In 1943, McPhee was in a depressive psychosis, having moved to New York and struggling to make a living, a sad contrast to the sustained euphoria of Bali, and he confessed to a psychiatrist: "Many times there was a decision to make between some important opportunity and a sexual (homosexual) relationship which was purely sensual. I never hesitated to choose the latter. The Balinese period was simply a long extension of this."

Yet his best years were those on the sexually ambidextrous island which inspired the two books, his lasting achievement.

Benjamin Britten

At 1,403 pages and at a cost of $125 for the boxed set, there are few gays who will be able to read "Letters From a Life: Selected Letters and Diaries of Benjamin Britten." One would hope that some day a publisher will edit it and produce a trade paperback edition, so inspiring is the story of the acclaimed British composer Britten's 40 year relationship with singer Peter Pears.

They met in 1937 and a year later "set up home together."

It was a casual intimacy that didn't yet involve the forsaking of all others.

In 1938 Pears said he was "running madly after a sweet tough Stage Hand but as usual I can't come to the point!"

As critic Paul Moor observes, "Their letters reveal two hot-blooded young men head over heels in love with each other." And their reciprocal ardor never seemed to cool, at least not on paper.

The letters are valuable from another perspective as well, as Stephen Greco notes, "An artist's life incorporates sexual identity, among many other factors, so biographies that leave out or disguise significant relationships make it very hard for readers, gay or straight, to assess how sexual identity may inform creativity. Artists who downplay their personal lives injure history's ability to understand their work."

In 1979, Pears said the letters were not the history of one man but "the life of the two of us. And that, it seems to me, is where I stand. I hope that some day we shall publish some of Ben's letters. I hope the climate will be right then for publishing some of the most marvelous letters that one can imagine, that he wrote to me." And that day, in 1991, arrived. Pears died in 1986.

J. Edgar Hoover: "I've Got a Secret"

Two books were released during the year to capitalize on the public's continuing fascination with longtime FBI director and professional blackmailer J. Edgar Hoover, an intriguing individual for gays because of the implicit overtones to everything we've found out about the man since his death in 1972.

And, as book reviewer Donna Minkowitz says, "The culture that could jail Pee-wee for wanking and yank 'Tongues Untied' off PBS hasn't come far from the defensively white-bread '50s that were Hoover's heyday.

"Sexual secrets in particular continue to command a high price in funds degranted, contracts withdrawn and (always) newspapers sold."

"There's something addicting about a secret," Hoover once said. And useful, too. In Curt Gentry's "The Man with the Secrets," it is revealed that the director forced favorable votes from Congress by blackmailing one lawmaker with a film of cocksucking and another with a tape of adulterous sex with a suspected Nazi.

The irony is that the man who hurt thousands of gays and lesbians over many years spent every dinnertime, weekend and vacation with his "constant companion," associate director Clyde Tolson, to whom he left the bulk of his estate. While Gentry is careful to point out that there is no proof of physical sex ever occurring between the two men, their relationship was clearly homoerotic. The life of the publicly puritanical director was actually full of relaxation, play and sensuality. "It's difficult," Minkowitz observes, "to know what to do with the knowledge that Hoover probably sucked cock."

What emerges from Gentry's book and Athan Theoharis' "From the Secret Files of J. Edgar Hoover," is that the director was more an opportunist than a political zealot. "Even when he did squash rebellions and enjoyments," says Minkowtz, "he seems to have done so not for its own sake put purely as a means to power. On many occasions, Hoover declined to bring his painstakingly collected data to light, preferring to blackmail offenders rather than curtail their behavior." President Harry S. Truman wrote in his diaries that Hoover's "polite blackmail" must stop, but it never did.

Hoover could be called "the premier outer of his day." He used his enemies' queerness as his chief weapon against them, deploying homophobia as a means to certain specific political ends. His methods were based on blaming and abasing individuals, not systems. Brilliantly manipulating both the print and electronic media so that there was nary a word of criticism about him for many years, it's about time Hoover got his due.

James Leo Herlihy

Valuable from an historical perspective, James Leo Herlihy was back on the best-seller lists during the year with reissues of two of his most famous works, "Midnight Cowboy" and "All Fall Down," books that made "bad boys" acceptable to the middle class.

"Unlike their uncredited sources, bad boys are not really bad," says the gifted writer and critic Gary Indiana, "bad boys are tourists of badness. The bad boy syndrome is overtly or secretly about conciliation and caring, even when it seems to be about icky, dirty things. It usually shows the weird, awful shapes people get twisted into by greed and lust and all the other cardinal sins. But bad boys can also be sweet-tempered and fascinated by benign oddities. The sense of the irremediable that hovers over the American landscape of Burroughs, Diane Arbus, and Douglas Sirk, the perception of doomed or blighted collective inanity conveyed by such disparate voices as Vidal and Nabokov run counter to the bad boy creed. Certain grotesqueries painted by these artists have iconic value in bad boy art, but not as paradigms of the big picture. For bad boys, America's flaws merely enhance its soft human features and democratic bedrock. Bad boys tell us, in one way or another, that there's no place like home."

In the early '60s when the Herlihy novels first appeared, he had achieved some fame as the author of the screenplay of "Blue Denim," what Indiana calls "a five-boner teen-pregnancy flick" and which starred one of my idols of the era, Brandon deWilde, who also starred in the screen version of "All Fall Down."

In 1991, Indiana maintains, one tends to view "Down" as a chronicle of male hysteria, that to avoid direct sexual contact between two brothers, a girl, impregnated by one of them, must die. In "Cowboy," Herlihy's hero Joe Buck grows up in the Southwest and emerges from the peacetime army with nothing to offer the world except his body, but plenty of people want it. He eventually gets the idea of selling it and he has at least one sexual encounter with a man that occasions little dread or embarrassment. Later on, though, in New York City, he comes to view gay sex as a sad, shameful business.

"The tourist motif of bad boy narratives," Indiana explains, "is especially strong in 'Midnight Cowboy:' Joe is in the world but not of it, menaced by exemplary monsters of nonfeeling, avarice, sexual mania and hypocrisy.

"Herlihy's novels are touching precursors of a cultural movement that has reinvented the closet, and patriarchal attitudes, with a vengeance that makes these books seem like comforting antiques."

Sex in Music

In the '70s, when noted music historian Jim Farber was in college, he covered rock groups for *Circus Magazine* and his mother, who taught sex education to alienated high school students in Yonkers, often had him speak to the kids.

"Unwaveringly," he recalls, "when it came time for Q&A, the kids asked the same sneering question: 'Which rock stars are gay?'

"'They all are,' I'd answer. 'Except for Freddie Mercury.'"

Years later, Farber still can't answer the question without performing a mass outing. "Despite the visibility and urgency AIDS has brought, you can still fit the number of 100% openly-gay-pop-stars-of-any-reasonable-stature snugly into one walk-in closet: Andy Bell, Jimmy Sommerville, Marc Almond, Tom Robinson, Phranc, the lead dorks in Frankie Goes to Hollywood, Gary Floyd of Sister Double Happiness, and Two Nice Girls and, I guess, Elton John and Boy George, if you discount that old 'bisexual' defense.

"No surprise, then, that every time some pop star leaps unequivocally out, the hearts of all true rock 'n'roll queens soar with possibilities. First, our aesthetic prayers: Will this finally be the one we won't have to pretend we like more than we do? Then the public relations concern: Is this the one who will do the supernatural and present an image that's at once butch/fem, retro/avant, quirky/average enough to represent the fullness of our 10%?"

Kitchens of Distinction

Patrick Fitzgerald of the Kitchens of Distinction won't be the one to make a difference but he is a start nonetheless. Patrick is the only openly gay member of the group, with two straights, so the band can't be considered a "gay group" but Patrick writes all the songs and sings them and decided that hot naked men should appear all over the cover of their debut album, "Love Is Hell."

Gay-themes pop up on only three of the 16 songs and the best of them, "Four Men," is, Farber criticizes, "moaningly similar to the work of everyone's favorite 'celibate,' Morrissey; the key line being, 'time to hate myself again.'"

Their new album, "Strange New World," has no naked coverboys and only a couple of songs that might be gay-themed. One, "Gorgeous Love," Patrick penned after his lover had been a victim of gay bashing outside a London leather bar. It contains the line, "I'm not ashamed of expressing the love I feel for you. It hurts to think this (gorgeous love) is seen as wrong."

If Fitzgerald is evasive onstage he hasn't been in interviews. "Perhaps he's most appealing," Farber says, "as a unstereotypical role model - both for the kind of music the group plays (you can't dance to it) and for his physical appearance (neither dashing or dismal, he looks like your average bohemian's idea of an everyday Joe). There's something in him that wants to stand out and be a hero."

In a recent interview he said that one of his "big things" is to "instill an idea of community and isolation. I want to feel that we're all in this together."

Perhaps he thinks the amiable hetero-homo mix in the band achieves that goal but such a utopian interpretation can only be achieved after the minority element has gained its full voice.

Helot Revolt

"Gay people have got to have something besides Judy Garland to commit suicide to," says Helot Revolt's manager. "The world's first openly faggot heavy-metal band" wears jock straps and fishnets, shows off phallic tattoos, plays air guitar, lip synchs and gives tabloid answers to tabloid questions.

As one reviewer commented, "There's performance art, there's heavy metal, and then there's when the two meet, with a result that's more enteratining than half the performance artists and half the metal groups in Southern California. I'd like to see more of these guys."

Helot songwriter, cutie Jack Spittle, says: "A lot of metal is homophobic, racist and sexist, and we want to have something for the guys who are rockers who get it on with other guys. It's time to bring overt queer consciousness to heavy metal."

"We just don't say 'fuck you' to our audiences," says John Maximum, swathed in heavy chains and leather rags. "It's 'Fuck you' and 'Fuck me.'"

On stage, they grab their cocks through their pants and sneer their Queer Nation anthem to the world: "Queers spreadin' out so far and wide/Keep team sports, just give me a man's backside."

Critic Doug Sadownick has revealed there is some confusion about how the group got together: "It's difficult to get a straight answer about Helot's origins. Spittle says they met in jail, arrested for masturbation in a popular West Hollywood sports club. Maximum says they tripped over each other's huge dicks at a sex club."

However they met, they continue to delight. Their new album is to be called "In Your Face, Up Your Butt" and the high point of their live performance is when they reincarnate Liberace to sing "We Are the Queers; We Want Your Children."

Now that takes guts.

Paul Lekakis

Though mentioned in Boze Hadleigh's "The Vinyl Closet" as "openly gay," Paul Lekakis plays it coy, perhaps to appease the subteen girls who are some of his biggest fans. His core audience are the club kids, the ones who go out every night and have a good time.

"A lot of people know me," he says, "and a lot of people know the way I am. The thing is, I don't like to come out and say anything because I don't know if I'll change my mind in a couple of years and I don't want to be labeled."

(Change his mind?)

"But I'm very open and I'm very free and I do exactly what I want to do. I'm cool about everything. "

Cool is putting it mildly. The handsome boy, who still models in his spare time, is a vision onstage: lithe, muscular, and blond, with a sweaty white T-shirt rolled up at the sleeves and cut-off gray sweatpants with obviously no underwear.

Spotted on the dance floor one night in New York by a pair of Italian record producers, he quickly won a recording contract and "Boom Boom" was the result, a song that went to number one in Australia and Japan and was a top ten dance tune in the U.S. He makes no apologies for the song's frank sexuality: "It's still valid. Sure, no one's going out and doing things the way they did five years ago, but everybody's still got that want and that passion. We're just doing it in different ways. And that's cool. You don't have to change your life. It's just being responsible and doing things about it. It's as simple as that."

Personally, he travels with his friends. "I'd rather teach my friends the ropes so I can have them near me so I can be happy. Life's too short not to be with people you care about."

Jimmy Sommerville

An unreconstructed leftist and militant gay activist whose greatest hits have been Dionysian dives into the disco canon of the '70s, Jimmy Sommerville is a longtime member of the British chapter of ACT-UP and never fails to walk his talk. "He is an indefatigable campaigner for his causes who makes himself available for countless benefit shows," says Steven Daly. "Forgive him then for not smiling at the irony of the video he made for the Cole Porter AIDS-benefit album, 'Red Hot + Blue,' was deemed too homoerotic for ABC's TV special."

Jimmy was "kind of upset," but not really surprised. "I just knew that it was going to be too controversial for them. But as a gay man involved in this project, it was important to do a homoerotic video. Because of AIDS, so many people are terrified at being told they've got to stop having sex. That's ridiculous - safe sex does exist; there is such a thing. So we showed passion and love and romance and emotion, because these are the kinds of things that have been affected by the whole crisis and the discrimination surrounding it.

"I don't speak for the gay community because a lot of gays hate what I do and think I'm too extreme. So I just speak for myself and always try to stress that. But I know there are people who think along similar lines and believe what I say. They appreciate that I have the opportunity to say things that they're not in the position to."

Speaking of being in an enviable position, Jimmy's fantasy is to be the unsuspecting pizza-delivery boy in a Jeff Stryker video. "He knows how to give people exactly what they want," Jimmy feels. "Jeff Stryker represents perfection, the American Dream."

(Now we know who's renting all those Stryker tapes!)

Gerardo

About "Rico Suave," Gerardo's debut video, Jim Farber says, "the guy's image is bloated enough to make the World Wrestling Federation look painfully withdrawn by comparison. Then again, Gerardo's egomania doesn't come entirely without credentials. As revealed in the video, his chest ripples with muscles, his face suggests a poignant mixture of sweetness and danger, and his rear end is shapely enough to send former MTV boy-toy George Michael back to the gym."

The video, which basically features the Ecuadorian-born dancer gyrating around, leering, is, Farber suggests, more than just a turn-on, it's a first: "No previous male star in video has presented himself in such completely fetishistic terms. Male dancers and featured players in videos may often get the raw meat treatment but with male stars, the camera focuses mainly on their faces, presumably to suggest a connection with their personalities. This is true even of lead singers from today's pop metal bands, who (from Jon Bon Jovi to Skid Row's Sebastian Bach) have in the age of video become almost miraculously cute.

"Gerardo suggests that he does little more with his life than take women to bed. By projecting only sex, Gerardo allows the camera to objectify his body entirely, turning him into nothing more than a remarkably useful object."

(Such an object. So useful.)

But the 26-year-old singer/dancer admits that he does have some flaws. Well, one anyway: "My ears stick out," he says. He describes himself as "Outgoing, ready to take chances, very energetic, always doing something," and he proved it when, after he moved to Glendale, California from Ecuador in 1976 with his parents, he set out to make something of himself. In the summer of his senior year in high school, "I got wild," he says. "I didn't want to deal with the books. But I knew I could dance and the girls loved it." He went on to win contests on "Solid Gold" and "Dance Fever," which led to roles in "Winner Take All," "Can't Buy Me Love" and "Colors." Even with the acting experience under his belt, he still had the music in him and he spent $9,000 of his own money to make a demo of that first video. A song producer liked what he heard, as well as what he saw, and Gerardo was on his way.

Contrary to what you might think, he does put his shirt on, most often when he sits down to dinner with his parents, with whom he still lives. But, to be truthful, he says "I look square in a shirt."

He also looks square without his trademarked head-wrapping, which he wears "to keep my hair from bugging me." He started with $3 hankies five years ago and now has worked his way up to expensive silk scarves, "I've been getting nice leather jackets and I try to find rags to match."

The dark-eyed charmer also admits he had a "late puberty" and in the 11th grade, too little for football and too short for basketball, he started lifting weights and wrestling. Nowadays, he stays in shape by practicing safe sex. Says he, "It ain't the meat, it's the motion."

Marky Mark

At 12, Marky Mark, the kid brother of Donnie Wahlberg, accused firebug and resident bad boy of the New Kids on the Block, was breakdancing on the street corners of Boston. A few years later, he was a part of the group, but he refused to take singing lessons and left. Now Mark is several million dollars poorer than his big brother but he's catching up, thanks to pop music catching up with his teenage hip-hop tastes. He had a big debut single, "Vibrations," and a great video, "Wildside," a vamp version of the Lou Reed classic, highlighted by beaucoup shots of Mark dressed carefully for public consumption: shirtless with his overalls undone, revealing his beefy muscles and the tops of his BVD's.

But he wants his fans to respond to his respect for the hip-hop art form, not his chiseled pecs. He realizes the street culture of the album shocks some people, "but that's how I am. My music is about more than just making money. It's about being true to myself and expressing my own feelings."

But he's enough of a businessman to hedge his bets, reports Gavin Edwards: "Recently, in the parking lot of a Ford dealerhip, Mark signs autographs. Girls shout, cry and unbutton their shirts for him. He's unflappable. Having seen his brother's success, Mark accepts the hysteria as a natural part of his job. He balks only when one girl asks him for his hat. No way. The hat's his sole sign of attitude: it leaves his face in shadow while dozens take his photo and it never leaves his head."

Gay New York columnist Michael Musto caught up with Mark at an MTV charity basketball game stripped down to only his underwear, prompting him to get some extremely good vibrations: "His briefs revealed much definition, apparently it's quite a funky bunch." A couple of weeks later, Musto reported, at the Ritz in the Big Apple, Marky got up to perform and turned into something from the gay strip joint Show Palace: "Shedding his jacket and strutting around bare-chested, later dropping his pants to reveal briefs tightly encasing what could only be described as a baseball bat. A waifish urchin no longer, he grabbed his crotch repeatedly and quipped, 'How's everybody in the motherfuckin' house doin' tonight?' Dancing and rapping like a demon, he barely remembered to pull the pants back up before stumbling offstage and hurting his knee. This guy makes Madonna's masturbation shtick look like an Anita Bryant orange juice commercial. The girls in the crowd went berserk, the guys booed." Well, not every guy.

Nelson

"They're beautiful!"
"They're great!"
"They're awesome!"

Those are some of the things you may hear at a Nelson concert. The blond-haired, blue-eyed twin sons of the late teen idol Ricky Nelson have become quite the heartthrobs in their own right, thanks to a number one hit, "After the Rain" and a sizzling video. "Once you rock with the twins, you'll never go back," as they say to their audiences at the end of their show.

They may look identical but they are really "mirror twins," which means they are opposites. "We're two halves of the same person," Matthew says, "We balance each other." Gunnar is more physical, emotional and unpredictable; Matthew is spiritual, romantic, intuitive. Matthew is the older Nelson (by 45 minutes; "Gunnar's always been a little difficult," jokes Matt). Gunnar is left-handed; Matthew right-handed. Matthew is passive, Gunnar active. "We are, without hesitation, each other's best friend," Matt says.

But they share the same vice: a taste for lust. Pelted onstage with panties and bras, and constantly propositioned offstage, they obviously have plenty of opportunities. Still, the thrill is slowly fading. "It's starting to get cheap," Matthew admits. Matthew's the monogamous one; Gunnar still likes to play around. But they share the same taste in clothes, ultratight jeans and low-cut or open shirts. They also share a disdain for drugs, having witnessed the havoc it caused in their own family with their mother and father. Says Matthew, "They were both so screwed up, it just had no romance or mystery for me. And I vowed I would never do it."

Three months after their 18th birthdays, their dad was killed in a plane crash. "We don't sing his songs. Nobody can do Ricky Nelson better than Ricky Nelson," Matthew says. "Anything we could do would be a parody. It would be disrespectful." They dedicated their first album to him.

In sum, their song from the soundtrack of "Bill and Ted's Excellent Adventure," says it all: "Two Heads Are Better Than One." Yum. Yum.

Sex in the Theater

"The nice part about things getting visibly worse is that people begin to notice how bad they are," Michael Feingold says. "As a result, they start to get better again."

The awful state of art (or life) doesn't improve overnight just because of its awfulness has become visible to the naked eye. "It takes time," Feingold says, "Shifts in consciousness occur bit by bit, causing shifts in practice that gradually solidify into a different way of doing things."

This can be said about how sex is treated onstage. Or how the reality AIDS is treated. This coalesced brilliantly in the popular playwright A. R. Gurney's "The Old Boy," presented in New York during 1991.

Over the years, the theme of a "different" boy and his problems at school has been presented as a matter of mere sensitivity, but, Feingold points out, is really one of sexual orientation. Popular entertainments such as "Young Woodley," "Les amities particulieres," "Tea and Sympathy," "A Separate Peace," "Dead Poets Society," and so on come to mind. In Gurney's play, the subject is not the tormented closet case but his straight best friend, who comes back to the school as a celebrated alumnus to give the commencement address, and learns his old friend has died of AIDS, causing him to come to terms with a lot of emotional conflicts.

While things were looking up on Broadway, a Dallas high school drama teacher was fired for staging "The Jerker," the late Robert Chasey's 1985 one-act play, which was sub-titled, "A Pornographic Elegy with Redeeming Social Value and a Hymn to the Queer Men of San Francisco in Twenty Telephone Calls, Many of Them Dirty." Director Bruce Coleman was fired for his efforts, even though the production was staged off-campus. A woman who didn't even have any children at the school brought the matter to the attention of the principal, claiming the play was "part of a conspiracy to overthrow the government and take over the Catholic Church."

Coleman claims the school knew what they were getting when they hired him. He had staged gay-themed plays before, such as

"Short Eyes" and "Bent." "They asked me how I went about choosing the plays I direct. I gave them every reason why I chose to do 'Jerker,' -politically, emotionally. One of the main reasons is because I'm tired of watching my friends die of AIDS. And that's probably one of the most Christian choices available - to help people see something that might keep them from dying."

In California, Michael Kearns acts on AIDS by acting. "My work equals AIDS activism," he says, and it's no self-serving remark. Richard Natale says that Kearns is "at the forefront of awareness of AIDS as a condition that knows no ethnic, sexual or class boundaries."

His passion began in the mid-'70s when he posed nude for the book "The Happy Hustler." The cover and full color inside centerfold, the first in a popular paperback, caused considerable stir and led to appearances on talk shows and his "coming out" to a nationwide audience, going so far as to say he was "happy being gay."

Although he has occasionally found work in some TV series, he says Rock Hudson's death has caused a whole new homophobic wave in Hollywood and he is now immersing himself in local gay theater. His first play, "Night Sweat", about AIDS, was produced to controversial critical response. "It filled a need that no one else had filled," he says. "It was staged in an outrageous fashion - vaudeville, burlesque, camp and soap opera -and it dealt with death in a sexy, horrific, funny and carnival way."

He expects to continue to write about AIDS because, "It's not going away in the near future; I won't be able to ignore it." His next project is an interracial AIDS story inspired by "Cyrano de Bergerac." Says the handsome, mustachioed 41-year-old star, "I'm not thinking in terms of money, but in terms of art."

Meanwhile, back on Broadway, Terrence McNally ("The Ritz") was back to his old tricks of using homosexuality to titillate the middle-of-the-road audience in "Lips Together, Teeth Apart."

"McNally doesn't bother to explore a gay character in detail," critic Guy Leslie complains. "In other words, make them operatic, make them horny, make them dead, but whatever you do, don't show a same sex couple behaving just like a hetero couple. No, the play seems to say, they are different from you and me."

Critic John Simon noted that the play "reeked with the suspicion of latent homosexuality in the heterosexual males, a favorite topic of McNally's."

The play is set on the deck of a Fire Island Pines beach house and two couples have arrived there to spend the Fourth of July weekend, during which one of the women must decide whether to keep the house, which she has just inherited from her brother, an AIDS victim. The gays are never seen as the play explores hetrosexual perceptions of homosexuality and AIDS. "But it's not an AIDS play, although the shadow of it informs the action," the author says. He adds that the gay society and straight quartet on stage "are not so different. Each side is looking at the other; they're each judging the other. But there is a gradual camaraderie. It's about coming to terms with mortality, and about being more forgiving."

Harvey Fierstein

Instead of bringing something new to Broadway, America' most famous gay man, Harvey Fierstein, ever inventive, re-staged the first "out" gay play ever presented, Robert Patrick's "The Haunted Host," circa 1964, to celebrate his 20th year in show biz. Last produced in 1975 with Fierstein in the lead, it is one of Patrick's best, according to his dear friend Quentin Crisp. "As always in Mr. Patrick's work," Crisp says, "the dialogue is full of puns so it may not be inappropriate to say that the action consists in trying to 'lay' the ghost."

Fierstein plays the middle-aged man who rents a room to a stranger, who turns out to resemble someone his host loved and who committed suicide. "Mr. Workman, who plays the guest," Crisp notes, "is youngish, tallish, slimmish, and blondish, thus fulfilling the sexual fantasies of the average homosexual man. But undoubtedly the evening belongs to Mr. Fierstein." As the evening always does when he's on stage. "I'm *the* homosexual!" he joyously proclaims in the play, and that's about right anywhere, anytime. The three-time Tony-award winning playwright/performer (for "Torch Song Trilogy" and "La Cage aux Folles") has by his own admission created a one-man cottage industry around a flamboy-ant public persona that declares, "I'm gay! I'm healthy! I'm happy!"

"It's important," he says, "for people to know that I choose to be openly gay and I'm not sad. And I choose a campy image because

I don't want the world to think I'm straight. That's not gay pride. I don't believe there is such a thing as gay pride. There's gay shame and normalcy. Did you know, it's supposed to be pronounced normalty?"

The 37-year-old plays himself as if he were "a well-loved onstage role," notes Simi Horwitz. "He revels in noting and commenting on everyone passing by in the street. It's all fodder for gossip and innuendo - from the busload of geriatric tourists pouring into an over-rated Chinese restraurant to the cute French sailor boys in their broad-brimmed hats to the matron in a peach-colored suit right out of a 1950s sci-fi flick sendup."

"I'm very private," Harvey says. "I'm very quiet. When my neighbors see me on a talk show they're surprised. They don't know me that way. They just know me as Harvey living his life."

That life consists of writing and performing every chance he gets. He starred in the film version of "Torch Song Trilogy," the hilarious "Garbo Talks," also with Anne Bancroft, and, for cable, "Tidy Endings," which won an ACE award. He narrated the Oscar-winning documentary "The Times of Harvey Milk" and he is the voice of Homer's secretary on "The Simpsons."

"Mostly," the star says, "I like to do stuff that makes me happy. My career is not as important as enjoying my life. I am a performer, not an actor. Actors are so busy with themselves, so self-important."

But being a famous performer, he has to live with a certain amount of controversy in his life, such as the wonderful moment when Harvey accepted the Tony award and thanked his lover.

"He does not suffer homophobia lightly," Horwitz says, citing the time on "Saturday Night Live" when guest host Kathleen Turner told actor Jon Lovitz playing Fierstein that his problem was that he'd never had a real woman. "That remark was offensive," says the star. "And I had a long meeting with the show's producers. They said that they were unaware that their skits were derisive to all gays. But they never did it again."

But he doesn't believe gays should be forced out of the closet. "Except maybe elected officials who are vehemently anti-gay and it turns out they're gay themselves. In other cases, it's nobody's business."

Tommy Tune

Gene Kelly told Tommy Tune when the Texan came to Holly-wood, "I understand that's your real name. Change it, it's too theatrical." But theatricality is what Tommy's all about.

While he didn't take Hollywood by storm, Tommy's succeeded on Broadway as few ever have, winning the Tony in 1991 as best director for his spectacular, very American musical "The Will Rogers Follies." The show was also named Best Musical and Tommy won for best choreography.

In a career that has been a series of mostly glowing reviews, he's the only artist to win Tony Awards in four different categories. In addition to his most recent awards, he won for Best Featured Actor in a Musical, "Seesaw" (1973), Best Choreography for "A Day in Hollywood/A Night in the Ukraine" (1980), Best Direction of a Musical for "Nine" (1982), Best Actor in a Musical, "My One and Only," which he also directed and won a Tony for choreography (1983), and Best Choreography and Best Direction of a Musical for "Grand Hotel" in 1989.

And in his own pixie-ish, gee-whiz way, Tommy's quite a sexy package. Michael Bennett, the Broadway dynamo who died of AIDS complications in 1987, thought so, too; there were rumors the two had been intimate, but it wouldn't have lasted, given Bennett's penchant for blue-eyed blond hustlers. Rock historian Boze Hadleigh said: "Privately, Michael's 'type' was WASPy blond, and his tendency was promiscuity. After he hit the heights with 'A Chorus Line' he married leading lady Donna McKechnie. Friends speculated he was 'going Hollywood,' some said he was using his wife as a 'beard' and Steve Rubell of Studio 54 fame claimed, 'Michael's trying for the impossible conversion.'" Later, after the divorce, Michael said, "Now I have matrimony in my resume." Cecil Beaton said: "Michael was the most driven man I've ever met, but he didn't enjoy it. He was half-Italian, half-Jewish, you know, and vascillated between being defiant about his homosexuality and hiding it. I had the impression he was unhappy without fame and fortune and that he was always trying to prove himself, wanting to fit in yet wanting to stand out."

"Michael and Tommy served up a perfect contrast of life in the eighties," Jeremy Gerard says. "While Bennett was burning the candle at both ends, Tune was dabbling in and ultimately retreating from the glitter scene. For him, the decade was a time of turning ever more inward spiritually. He pared his life to the essentials."

"Of course," Tommy says, "you go through life sampling, but I didn't get the trip of the designer drugs. The ritual I understood, and the back-roomness of Studio 54 and all that. I liked the glamour and the secretness of it, but it was a vacant thrill."

"Anatomically he's like four Fred Astaires laid one on top of the other," raves Charles Marowitz about the skyscraping 6-foot-6 star, "giving new meaning to the hackneyed phrase, 'tripping the light fantastic.' Resembling an anthropomorphic maypole, there is something truly fantastical about his elongated stage presence and the way he conveys the 'lightness' of snow melting on a windowpane or summer drizzle augmenting the surface of a pond."

Besides finding Tune attractive, Bennett also knew talent when he saw it and gave the boy his chance in a supporting gay role in "Seesaw."

But it is as a director that Tune has achieved his greatest fame. He had his first hit with "Best Little Whorehouse in Texas." What he did with all those tall, sexy cowboys was phenomenal. But Hollywood thought of him as "too light" to direct the screen version and gave the job to Colin Higgins, who died of AIDS in 1988. The film, starring Burt Reynolds and Dolly Parton, although fun, set no boxoffice records.

Tommy admits to being born over 50 years ago (can you believe it? Must be all the yoga and breathing exercises he does every morning) in Wichita Falls, Texas and his voice still carries a touch of that Texas twang, adding a friendly lilt to his words. In conversation, he's quick to register intrigue, concern, abashment, sympathy, or disdain on a fairly restricted facial palette. "It's the ephemeral presence of life as it is and how precious it is," Gerard notes.

The star usually has at least three shows in development and maintains a hectic schedule. "I don't use very much sleep," he says. "It's not necessary. That's something I did when I was younger. But when you grow older and you realize how precious life is...you don't want to waste it sleeping."

"You know," says William Ivey Long, who designed the costumes for "Nine," "there are two ways you can do the story of

Tommy Tune. You can either do a glorification of this great American genius or you can dish him. Everything one says about Tommy is quirky; you can't say something ordinary about him. In addition to being mad as a hatter, he drop-kicks you into dreamland." And we can't think of a nicer place to be!

The Gallery:
The Best of the Superstars
1992: The Year in Sex

Keanu Reeves
Photographed by Brad Pierce

Robert Downey Jr.
Photographed by Karen Kuehn

Brad Pitt
Photographed by George Holz/Onyx

Director Todd Haynes
Photographed by Steve Warren

Rupert Everett
Photographed by Greg Gorman

Billy Warlock

Jason Priestley

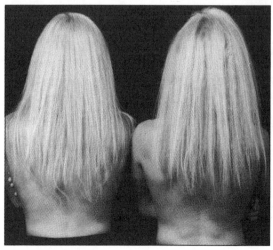

Nelson: Matthew and Gunnar

Marky Mark
Photographed by Spike Nannarello/Shooting Star

Gerardo

Ryan Idol
Photographed By Stuart Rosenburg

Ryan Yeager and Chad Knight
at an autograph party in Hollywood

Book II.
The Best of the Stars of Video Erotica

"Big Tom Steele"

"The three basics are the face, the body and the dick. You can get away with having two of them, or if your cock is abnormal enough in size, then just one will do. People really want to see those big dicks."

— *Golden Age Pornstar Luke*

Introduction: Sex For Sex's Sake

"I've managed to live up to being 'Luke,' yet I remain obscure, remain myself," said the boy known as Luke, one of early porn film pioneer Jack Deveau's major stars of the '70s. "Luke has a following, but he's no Kip Noll. I can walk down the street and keep his secret. And I can remember that Luke gave a lot of people a lot of happy moments. That makes me happy."

Happy Luke's favorite role, I kid you not, was in something called "Times Square Strip," which is as tasty a morsel now as it was then, then being what some of us oldtimers refer to as the "Golden Age of Porn," an age that began in the early '70s, when gay erotic cinema was largely restricted to films which unspooled at a small number of big houses in major cities. The theaters demanded a constant stream of product and although most of it, produced largely in New York, is unwatchable today, there remain some classics, including many of Deveau's works and Wakefield Poole's "The Boys in the Sand" and Terry Le Grand's S&M "Born to Raise Hell," the first gay erotic flick to be reviewed in *Variety*, the show business newspaper and one of the two gay erotic films that are part of the permanent collection at the Museum of Modern Art in New York City, the other being Fred Halsted's "Sextool."

In the late '70s, the scene moved to Los Angeles and with the premiere of William Higgins' "The Boys of Venice" at the Century Theater in 1978, a new kind of gay eroticism was born. The film featured decidedly young performers romping around in luxurious bedrooms, seductive ski lodges, and gorgeous mansions with swimming pools. Later, they travelled to exotic locales such as Hawaii and Aspen for sex so hot it consumed the screen.

But it took Andre Blay, who put the first feature films on videocassette, to make such wonderful diversions available to the masses. With a VCR, every gaymale in the world could enjoy what had been only a pleasure for big city folk. The trouble with the phenomenal growth of video was that, by the mid '80s the producers had been hit with a technological future shock. As the sales of VCRs burgeoned and erotica was rented by the day by the masses, attendance at adult theaters and mail order sales dropped substantially. The box office income that created big profits and made possible the underwriting of adult movies vanished. The producers of erotica found themselves having to increasingly depend on the sale of videos to retailers, who can rent the same film dozens of times. The potential for better films with characterization, story lines and better acting was suddenly derailed in favor of turning out as much product as possible as swiftly as possible, with a threadbare budget. Soon we were back in the dark ages of porn. The situation was exacerbated by the advent of direct-to-video. Now everyone with a camera could get into the act.

But despite the poor quality, demand for erotic video continued to mushroom. According to a survey conducted in 1990 by *The Adult Video News*, the industry's trade magazine, 68% of the video stores in the country carried adult titles, up 8% from two years earlier.

In those stores, the percentage of sales and rentals that come from erotic films was over 20%. The percentage of erotic-film customers who want films depicting men with other men was 13%. Male/female couples account for 29%, men alone 40% (an astounding figure, accounting for the growth in the male stripper-type video category), women alone 15%, and women with other women, 3%.

Beginning in the mid-'80s, AIDS was casting a sinister pall over the industry and it had been hoped that the advent of a health crisis so severe would give way to more romantic stories, a return to the narrative form that was so endearing in the mid-'70s, but it seldom happens. "These days with the burgeoning video market promising big bucks," renowned film critic Ted Underwood observed, "skin flicks are being turned out faster than cars off the assembly line in Detroit. This mass market approach follows standard conventions: bring together a group of attractive sex machines, mix them together in varying arrangements, permit no more than thirty seconds of clumsy, improvised dialogue to introduce them, quickly race through the conventional paces of manual, oral and anal activity, record myriad close-ups of quivering sphincters and twitching phalluses, and be sure to include at least two cum shots per performer. Cover the action with at least three cameras, alternate indoor and outdoor settings, contrast blonds with brunettes and new faces with old, hype the proceedings with pulsating score to compensate for the mechanical rutting, and sixty to ninety minutes later, fade to black with or without any indication that the product has reached its conclusion. In the right hands, these conventions can make electrifying erotica. But too often these days, there is no guiding hand, no master vision, to give the work shape, meaning, empathy, and, most of all, sexual heat."

But, as Golden Age pornstar Luke observed, "Art doesn't sell as porn. Greasy, dirty sex sells. The porn customer will tell you, 'Art is nice but it doesn't make me come.' Art brings compliments, not money."

While art for art's sake is a usually a turn-off, sex captured in a artful manner can give off the greatest charge of all. Years back, Brad Gooch asked: "Can a porn movie be a bad movie? People tend to go to porn theaters mostly for that 'larger picture' (the experience of being there) of which a review could only be written by a god." Those days, with things so busy in the theater itself, most guys really didn't pay much attention to what was going on on the screen. With rare exception, I know I didn't. But it is those rare exceptions that we concern ourselves with here. The purpose of this review is to celebrate the guiding hands, the master visions, and the performers who generate the sexual heat that is so elusive these days, the creme de la creme of gay male erotica, proving that sex for sex's sake need not be dull. It's the kind of heat that, if you fast-forwarded through it, you'd burn up your remote control.

Note: In addition to our own correspondents from "the field," the critics cited herein include the esteemed David Kinnick, who writes for the *Adult Video News* and *The Advocate;* long-time observers of the video scene John Rowberry and Aaron Travis, writing for *Adam Film World* and *Adult Video News;* Sid Mitchell, editor of the gay section of *The Adult Video News;* the staff of industry reviewers at Jerry Douglas' *Manshots Magazine;* and Mickey Skee, editor of *Gay Video Guide.*

The Best of the Super Sex Stars

It was the noted sex researcher Alfred Kinsey who found that a fully erect male averaged only two-and-one-half minutes of thrusting after penetration. And statistics show that the average male member is a little less than six inches in length when erect. No, when all is said and done, the average male just wouldn't make it in Hollywood. As Luke commented, "The three basics are the face, the body and the dick. You can get away with having two of them, or if your cock is abnormal enough in size, then just one will do. People really want to see those big dicks."

As for objective standards, Rick & Dave, the boys out at *Frontiers* in Los Angeles said it best: "Dudes: They gotta be hot. Dicks: They haveta be hard. Dialogue: There better be some."

Jeff Stryker, Ryan Idol and Lex Baldwin, et. al.
The Men We Love to Hate

Here come Jeff Stryker and more inheritors to his throne as the top of the tops. We've heard about them for years. Ever since Jeff came to power, and what an awesome power it is, in 1983, there's been a new challenger every year. These are the guys we love to hate. And they are few and far between. As William Higgins said: "A good top is hard to find. When someone can always top and never have a problem, you don't mess with success."

When considering the industry's awesome, generally insatiable tops, editor and producer Jerry Douglas often ponders the dichotomy: negative responses far outweigh the positive, yet the videos sell and rent like crazy, with swaggering Jeff remaining the ultimate example of the man we love to hate. If you're going to pay homage to a straight persona, you've gotta hate it. It's a phenomenon deeply rooted in the gay psyche. We hate these guys who seem to slide so easily through life, slipping between the thighs of men and women alike. How can they do this, some ask. Some of us who have been there just like guys more than girls and stick to it, opportunities aside. But with these guys, you never know. And that's the basis of their mystique.

Director Higgins was responsible for introducing several of the hottest tops in the business, all with better than average endowment, including Kip Noll, Rick Donovan, Michael Christopher and J. W. King. One that eluded him, however, was Jeff Stryker. "You know," Higgins has said, "when you're in the business, you're always talking about the one that got away. Jeff Stryker was more or less like this because we always wanted to find somebody perfect to shoot with him. So he sat around waiting for a year and we didn't get nearly as much work done with him as we should."

What "work" that did get done was spectacular indeed and now Jeff continues to wow 'em. His "On the Rocks" exploded on the market as an instant top-seller and features one of the best three-ways of the year, if not of all time. Jeff is matched with hot newcomers Joey Stefano and Matt Gunther. A fan in Georgia wrote, "Jeff kisses Joey! Incredible!"

Later, Joey was to dish Jeff, as only Joey can (as told to R. Couri Hay): "To begin with, he's short. His dick isn't as big as it looks, and he has a lot of difficulty getting it all the way up. I'm sure I don't have to tell you that he's not too bright. (The reader should know that Stefano is not a rocket scientist during the day.) The worst part of making a film with Jeff is the sex. I mean, I had to go home and have sex with someone else to get off." (Whoa! It sure looked like you were enjoying it - and whose cum was it anyway?)

Straight porn starlet Robin Byrd disagrees. She told Chi Chi La Rue that Jeff was "as big as you think." She should know; the two made their own home video in Robin's room during the electronics convention in Las Vegas.

So the controversy continues to swirl around the stud with the boyish face, perfect body, and long, fat, incredibly juicy cock that won't quit coming (he's usually good for two "money shots" per appearance), all combining to send sales of Stryker videos through the roof since he hit the screen.

After being "discovered" in Matt Sterling's "Bigger Than Life" sequel to "Inch by Inch," Stryker made several punchy flicks under the aegis of John Travis, then struck out on his own. It is often said that good friends Travis and Sterling co-developed the Stryker persona, shaping him as well as his career. Stryker came to Hollywood from the Midwest wanting to be a porn star but having no idea how to do it. Going so far as becoming a lover to both Sterling and Travis at various stages of his career, Stryker succeeded because, as Travis put it, "he was in tune with doing this. So many models today have the opportunity but are too busy doing other things. Stryker was dedicated to quality and building himself up." And, Sterling says, Jeff had that special gift great true film stars have: when the camera rolls, they exude charisma. Just hanging out with these pros, he learned from them and he took advantage of the knowledge they freely gave him.

Part of the Stryker mystique is holding back, not reciprocating, because Travis feels that if one lays all of one's cards on the table at once, there is no mystique. "Creating an illusion, creating a fantasy - that's basically what we're selling."

The Stryker message became sex as punishment, fulfilling a fantasy, taking to the extreme the idea of the "straight" stud who doesn't mind giving a gay guy a thrill. Erich Lange said: "He's a good fuck, a strong top." And until "Stryker Force," in which he kissed a man twice, he never showed much affection for those willing men he assaulted. Typical of his method is the sequence in "A Portrait of Jeff Stryker," from 1987, which later was incorporated in the first episode of a 1989 Catalina release called "The Look." Herein, Jeff is running a garage and he takes two younger fellows, Ricky Turner and Kevin Wiles, at the time two of the industry's workhorse bottoms, into his place of business and disciplines them for breaking a windshield. He makes them suck his cock and then, after he fucks each of them and throws a copious load, he lets the boys overhear a phone conversation. It is then they realize he knew all along they didn't break the windshield and they stand gaping as he hangs up the phone and grins mischievously at them.

It is in this episode that we are treated to one of Jeff's patented raunchy monologues. In a recent book by Brian Pronger, "The Arena of Masculinity," attention is called to Stryker's verbal commentary: "A typical monologue Stryker delivers in a tough, low voice is: 'Fuck him in his mouth,' 'Take all that big cock,' 'Choke on that big motherfucker,' 'Watch him suck that big dick,' 'Fuck him with that big dick - he likes that,' 'Stick that big cock all the way up his ass; pound it in him, pound it in him.' While the language is, to say the least, coarse and the sexual activity brutal, the recipients of Stryker's masculine ministrations are always very appreciative; this is not surprising since the scenes are such overwhelming incarnations of homoerotic paradox. After he has commented on his own masculine force, Stryker will draw attention to the joy of his partner by pointing out the rapture of the same: 'You like that big cock going up your ass don't you? Huh?' 'He likes that, don't he? See, he's got a big ole hard-on.'"

Pronger left out a few of our favorite Stryker directives, namely:

"Suck that big dick," "Lick my butt," and, of course, finally, "Tighten that asshole!" Jeff said that in the beginning the directors just let him go crazy. "I wasn't guided," he said, "I wasn't pushed." And Matt Sterling confirmed this, saying the dirty talk was totally unrehearsed, undirected: "It came forth so willingly, so excitingly."

If one looks at these bouts as competition, on rare occasions, while letting Stryker think he's always "on top," "punishing" a boy's butthole to the best of his ability, a bottom may actually win the game. Consider the scene in "Stryker Force" with Robert Harris. Stryker offers himself and his huge cock up to the pliant Harris, who, from the looks on his face throughout the sequence, is having a helluva lot more fun than Jeff. And, by taking every inch of that meat, Harris is, in effect "castrating" the stud, bringing him down.

Higgins told Jerry Douglas that Stryker's creators believe that the only person gays are really interested in viewing is "the quintessential top man who is essentially trade and is insulting to the gays. And you know I can play along with that when I feel like it, but I don't think it's a persona that I find attractive. I think that Stryker, more than any model I've ever known, generates more positive and more extremely negative comments than any other model. And you know, I don't find anything attractive or sexual about his screen persona." Director Jeff Lawrence agrees: "Stryker is the ultimate effort in the thinking that the heterosexual is the epitome, stationed above us and forever unattainable. It pisses me off. Sex is, after all, sex, and I really do think that regardless of who is participating it brings us all down to a common level."

Indeed, Jeff got more common than he's ever been in "Powerfull 2," his own sequel to "Powertool," by nibbling a bit on Alex Stone's cock. And since he has steadfastly refused to get fucked on screen, many stars would like to be the first to do it. Andrew Michaels (star of "Buddy System II"): "You know what I'd like to see and what a lot of people would like to see, is me fuck Stryker. I mean, he's already going down on people. I think that would sell a lot of copies: when Stryker gets it! And I think I should be the one to do it! I think it would be the best scene ever!"

The first flick produced, directed and edited by Jeff was "Every Which Way," with Nick Elliot ably serving on camera. But it's the little "public service" message about condoms that he tacks on the end that we could have done without. It may be in keeping with his on-screen persona but blowing smoke rings and saying he needs a Gladbag instead of a condom, when added to the fact that one of the girls in the video says, "Take that rubber off and fuck me," is true theater of the absurd.

During the year, Jeff finally got it together in the straight video arena with his own production, "Cummin' Together." Paired again with Jamie Summers, Jeff features what reviewer Mark Kernes described as "one of the best sex scenes I've ever seen." The action takes place around a pool and under its little waterfall and boasts underwater photography *ala* the old Higgins films. Jeff also gets to play a milkman in one sequence. (Talk about typecasting!) Straight or not, it's a don't miss for diehard Stryker fans.

In one interview, Jeff revealed that he thought what he was doing was "morally wrong." He knows he's a "sinner" like everyone else but doesn't "choose to hide his sins." Yet, in his interview with *Interview Magazine* when asked whether he was happy in porn, he replied: "I don't think there's anything wrong with the movies I do. They're made to entertain people. I'd like to venture out of pornography. Maybe do a couple more videos, then go on to something with a wider audience. And just grow, basically. Because I got into pornography hoping it would be a stepping stone. If Traci Lords can do it, I can too. And I don't even think she can act. If I could get a major motion picture, I'd rely on my acting ability rather than my name. Because I do feel I can act. I've done a pretty good job of it so far, even though I've never taken acting lessons. I've been told that I'm a little like Brando or Dean. I don't know, though. I can't see that when I look in the mirror."

What he can see in the mirror is that fabulous cock. The stud told Michael Musto that his cock has "a mind of its own. It's unisex. I like it and it likes me and we get along fine. It earns its own income. In fact, it supports me. Who's the smart one here?"

You better believe it. Besides that infamous dildo, there's now a complete line of Stryker sex products, including lube, playing cards, the pump and the "How to Enlarge Your Penis" video at $19.95. The world's best-selling dildo was molded from his magnificent cock by Doc Johnson. Jeff said: "They added nothing in width but they added an inch in length. It insults me that they did that." He also has a nonsexual instructional video, "Strike Back Vol. 1," obviously aimed at gays who are sick of gay-bashing and want to learn about karate self-defense technqiues. The muscular stud spends most of the hour-long running time topless so John Conlin said he doubted that the viewers of the tape would be practicing what Jeff was preaching. Rather, they would be opting for the "one handed chicken-choking hold." In other words, some guys can get off watching good ole boy Jeff do anything at all.

Jeff's advice to guys wanting to get into porn? "Stay home and go to school." Smart guy, this.

To catch this phenomenon at his very best, definitely include scenes in "Powertool," "In Hot Pursuit," "Stryker Force," "The Switch Is On," and the hetero "Jamie Loves Jeff," ("Jamie Loves Jeff 2," made by Stryker himself bombed with critics) and the solos: "Portrait of Jeff Stryker" and "Jeff Stryker: A Romance Video for Women," which features the "Portrait" stuff plus the lengthy, very hot shower sequence from "The Switch Is On," perhaps the quintessential Stryker solo scene, showing how comfortable Jeff is in the nude. In fact, he told Musto that he'd feel more comfortable if he could conduct his interviews in the nude as well: "Usually when people come in and take their clothes off, I like them. Yep, but once I wrestle somebody and throw them around a few times, get to know them, get in a few of their orifices -I'm more comfortable." Aren't we all?

*

One connoisseur of he-man action wrote, "I fast-forwarded through Ryan Idol's 'Score 10' except for his final scene. He's one of the best straight, gay-for-pay guys. He has a sense of mischief and fun. The funniest thing about the scene was the incredible lengths the cameramen went to to verify Idol didn't need a stunt dick to do his penetrating for him."

The reason for this care, obviously, was because of the brouhaha caused by rumors that porn vet David Ashfield had stunt-dicked Idol in his first gaymale feature, "Idol Eyes," directed by Matt Sterling, wherein Ryan was asked to fuck Joey Stefano. (Hey, guys, maybe Ryan just felt, Look, this kid's had every cock in the world up there, and all kinds of stuff besides, who knows? Hey, stunt it for me.) But Ryan insists that he didn't have any trouble with Joey. "I get off if the other person is really into me, really gaga. That's the way Joey was. He's a great kid, and I liked him a lot because he really dug me. We did things when the cameras weren't on; I wish we could have taped them." (Boy, so do we!) Ryan laments the outcome, or lack of same: "It was my first. I was petrified. I'll get better each time."

For "Score 10," Sterling's friend and co-worker John Travis said that he didn't like to "break the illusion" by showing the mechanics of applying a rubber, but that they were very concerned about taking every precaution. The latex decisions on the video were left up to the performers. "In the scenes between Ryan and Dcota and between Mike Henson and Dolph Knight, it was their choice not to use rubbers. But we absolutely insist on spermicide." (Interestingly, Mike Henson made his comeback in Jerry Douglas' prize-winning "More of a Man," topping Joey Stefano, and the rubber he used on the infamous ass was the final shot in the film.)

Dave Kinnick summed up the Idol phenomenon (and "Score 10") succinctly: "Idol locks in his screen persona as gay video's favorite beautiful, arrogant and superficial ass-wipe." Kinnick objects to these hostile, straight-trade attitudes. "Idol is not the cause of this malaise, but merely a symptom of the affliction. At the end of the video, we leave Idol smirking into the camera lens and telling us (and co-star Dcota) that he had 'a good time.' It is the very picture of a man absolutely dedicated to his own desperate specialness."

Speaking of specialness, the most lovingly produced video featuring Idol is "Ryan Idol: A Very Personal View," produced by his agent, Stuart Rosenberg (also known as the physique photographer Troy Saxon). Although violating the first rule of stardom by introducing us to the man behind the image before creating one, this ego trip is worth the journey for the stud's playfulness during a photo shoot sequence. It is an endearing moment. And early on Ryan sets the tone by saying he likes to hold off until he can't stand it any more and that's how you feel waiting for something to happen. Eventually, it does, first at Studio One in L.A. where he shows off for the crowd in a loose black g-string that leaves little to the imagination and then, totally naked, he shakes his pretty appendage and strokes it to the delight of the crowd. At one point, he gets a guy to sit in a chair on stage and proceeds to climb over him, shoving his ass in the guy's face. "I love the power of performing," he tells guest star Steve Hammond, another of Stuart's proteges, before retiring to the mirrored bedroom to talk to the camera as he jacks off. His dialogue is inspired: "You want some hard cock?" "Just picture it any way you want it." "Goddam that feels good." "I like someone who can bring me to the point and then stop, then bring it back again and again. I know you know what I'm talking about." "You wanna see this big cock come?" "Hey, you want me to come now?" After he shoots he says, "Such a pretty mess, eh?" "Ah, that was so incredible. Hmmm." Got that right, Ryan.

Ryan is less magnificent in his personal appearances. Recalls Michael Musto of *The Village Voice*: "Hundreds fell silent at the Dallas' Men's Room when porn star Ryan Idol - who looked as if he was covered in mayo or something-begging us to ask him personal questions as he ground his pelvis into the night. 'Andy Warhol said everyone will be in the spotlight for 15 minutes,' he told us, tauntingly. 'This is your chance.' You mean my big break was going to be in a dank, smoky nightclub interrogating a porn star about his oral/anal preferences? I'd hoped for something just a tad more glamorous, like sucking eyeballs out of fish heads on public access TV."

So what are those oral/anal preferences? When asked if he was straight, gay or in-between, the stud replied, "None of the above. I really don't label myself. I feel I could fit in anywhere- no pun intended. There are people who would like me to be straight and people who would like me to be gay. If I say one or the other it ruins their fantasies."

During the year, Ryan made his first straight video, "Letters from the Heart," and seemed to be having a rigidity problem. AVN reviewer Pearl Chavez: "Idol gets his tired marriage sparked by his exotic teddy-clad wife Leilani. Although he struggles with rigidity at times, Idol is so gorgeous that this is easily forgotten." Maybe by you, Pearl, but while we forgive, we never forget and this film proved to us that Ryan needs a man around to service that big thing the way it ought to be serviced. Thus, Ryan's first bi-sex movie can't be far behind.

Also during the year, Ric Bradshaw directed Ryan in "Idol Worship," an aptly named and imaginative AVG release. Sid

Mitchell comments: "Ryan's arrogant, almost parodic imitation of Jeff Stryker has never been put to better use than in the opening solo of this pseudo military tale of life on a submarine patrol in the Indian Ocean. As the sub's commanding officer, Idol's arrogance seems not only believable but even appropriate, and for once, highly erotic. He j.o.'s while commanding his crew to keep their eyes on the radar screens.

"As for the rest of the video, Blade Thompson easily steals the show, first with Domino in the torpedo chute, then with Rick Lee in their bunk." There is plenty of heat in every scene, making up for the absurdity in the connecting footage.

A stud who stands 6'1" tall and weighs in at 190 lbs., Ryan spends a lot of time at the gym but he doesn't consider himself a body-builder. "I'm a body sculptor," he says. "I build everything that should be built to achieve the perfect physique." And then there's the perfect cock that's 8 1/2" at full strength (about which *Manshots* magazine commented, "His groin looks as if it were cut by a master gemsmith."), which seems to get a good workout as well, since he has two lovers, an older one and a younger one: "If the older one can't fill the shoe, the younger one gets to." And poor Ryan, like the rest of us mere mortals, is getting older by the day and, he says, that means less sex. "Two or three times a day, that's it." Gives one pause, doesn't it?

*

"Man of the Year?" "Lex who?" Another fan: "He put me off with all his pseudo-trade bullshit. He looks good in print ads but he's a real loser."

As *Contax* magazine's reviewer put it, "I'm lukewarm on the way Lex is being packaged as the heir to Jeff Stryker in that he's always a top and never reciprocates the sex that's lavished on him. It's just too cold a persona for me. Lex is hot to ogle. He's kind of short, but his dick commands attention when it's randy and looking for a hole to fill."

Which is, if his videos can be believed, often. We first saw the luscious Lex in "Straight to Bed," Catalina's compilation of sup-posedly straight studs jerking their meat for a presumably gay audience.

Critic Sid Mitchell thought Lex looked uncomfortable, overcompensating with almost parodistic posturing and comical attempts to be "sexy," but *Manshots* raved: "The fifth performer, Lex Baldwin, appears on a motorcyle clad in a leather jacket and Levis. (He) displays a special talent for raunch raps as he speaks into the camera amd we believe him. He tells us how hard his dick is and we see he is telling the truth. As he jerks his cock, his hips gyrate forward and his face is filled with an intense look of pleasure that is unforgettable. When we first see him fully naked, standing in front of the motorcycle, still clad in leather boots, we immediately notice his entire pubic region is shaved bare. Several expert shots allow us to examine his entire body, including his beautiful ass, the crack of which he even fingers at several points. His orgasm is punctuated by loud grunts and groans, his juice dripping below onto the leather seat of the motorcycle." Can't please everyone.

In "Man of the Year," Lex continues to try to out-Stryker with his sex talk: in the truck stop tearoom scene, as he slides his glassy cock in and out of a gloryhole he cries, "Yeah! Suck that trucker's dick. C'mon, make it feel good." If only truckers really looked and acted like this! And tearooms should be so squeaky clean! As Dave Kinnick reports, "Building the better part of an entire video around a highway rest stop tearoom is a fine idea. On the other hand, shooting the whole thing in what is glaringly a tearoom set isn't the way to do it. If ever realism is called for, this needs it. The standing set (also used in "Loaded" and "Pacific Coast Highway II") is an overly pretty, two-wall construction with a pair of flimsy dollar ninety-eight stalls and a couple of non-functional household toilets. It looks like they had Mary Richards in to distress the set's features. And, as usual, tearoom protocol is thrown out the window as the performers roam around the room buck naked, confident that no one can come in to interrupt their activities since, after all this is a soundstage somewhere in Tarzana." But despite the surroundings, the *Contax* magazine reviewer went into orbit over this video: "Get this straight, once and for all, Lex is the star. All the other guys are secondary to Lex. Have you got that? I've fallen in line, too. I just can't get enough of the big lug. Lex enters the lavatory dressed in a grey pullover and tight jeans. He steps into a stall and closes the door. He sits down on the immaculately clean toilet seat cover and taps his foot while waiting for someone to follow him into this (trashy) bathroom. Next in the space is Christopher David. He's in super tight jeans and a green muscle-tee. He's looking very hot. David sits in the adjoining stall and waits a few beats before pulling a wad of toilet paper from the glory hole between the stalls. Lex gets interested and pokes his fat 'ole pecker through the hole and David lunges for it with quivering lips. Someone could have used a wider drill bit for this hole 'cause Lex has it filled. Woof!" Woof indeed.

After watching Lex fuck the hell out of David in "Man of the Year," we all wanted to see this "straight" man fuck a woman so Catalina obligingly let us have "Sex Bi-Lex," directed by Josh Eliot, a little bit of fun that also featured the normally hetero humping Jon Dough, hunky Chance Caldwell and Danny Summers.

Mickey Skee: "Anything with Lex Baldwin has got to be good. He's a brown-eyed, tight-bodied white stud who usually slicks back his hair and is slightly hairy all over his body. We hope he will develop more of a personality in future vids."

Later in the year, "Power Tool 2" was released and as Sid Mitchell comments, "Unfortuantely Lex Baldwin is a pale substitute (for Stryker). His scenes with Henson and Converse are as stale as last week's bread." He may be bland in action but in a still, well, Lex, who is hetero sex star T.T. Boy's brother, is on the boxcover in Levis, indiscreetly showing the admirable head of his cock. Since he's handcuffed to jail bars, it's a "Don't we wish!" pose that never appears in the movie and Lex just looks luscious.

*

Gayporn maven Chi Chi La Rue (aka Taylor Hudson) has said of Ryan Yeager, "He was a director's dream come true. Flawless! In his very first scene he gave me two cum shots, got fucked and bit a chunk out of a ladder." Talk about studmeat!

While some will tell you that performing sex on screen lowers their self-esteem, prostituting themselves, Ryan gets an ego boost out of it. "It is nice to be appreciated for what you look like and for what you are doing. It's flattering - and good money. I enjoy being part of what is such a big part of gay life, the whole pornographic industry. I'm fascinated by the business, actually. It has such a diverse group of people working in it."

But it's not Ryan's career; he lives a quiet life, has a thing with Tony Erickson (who started his porn career as Tony Sinatra and who was so memorable in "Secret Boys Club" with his dick laid between hot dog buns and who also has a thing for Damien), and has a "seven-to four job with a very conservative company in San Diego." Working nights and weekends, he gets the job done. For a hobby, he's done well. His videos have included the hit "Davey and the Cruisers," "Air Male," "Buddy System," "Buddy System 2," "Fond Focus," "The Rise," and "Powertool 2."

Ryan thinks of himself as the all-American boy-next-door, very sensual but not fucking everything he sees, with a softness to him. Sid Mitchell says Ryan is one of the few performers whose sum total spells "super star:" "...Sexual versatility that is delightfully surprising, a winning way with dialogue and the rare ability to stay in character even during sex scenes."

Like Joey Stefano, Jason Ross and numerous others, Ryan credits La Rue for his success. "He's a very dear friend at this point. We've really become close. He allows me to pick who I want to work with." Even though he's attracted to a guy as a partner, if he's into drugging or drinking, no thanks. "Someone just starting out needs an advisor like Chi Chi, someone who knows the ins-and-outs."

If anyone knows the ins-and-outs it's Ryan: "Safe sex can be just as sexy as unsafe sex. People are becoming so accustomed to it, I don't even think it bothers them. They don't even notice it a lot of times. My sex is hot, wholesome, and very basic. There has to be great sensuality amd there has to be a lot of kissing. Kissing is such an erotic and sensual part of sex and so underrated in gay video.

"In what most people find sexy, laughter is not involved. But the movie that I won best supporting actor for ("Stranded") I played a real bitch. It was so much fun playing a charcter that wasn't really me. I got in a fight with the person I ended up having sex with and it all ended up in laughter."

The stud meets his match in Catalina's "Headstruck" with Jason Ross giving him marvelous head and then jacking him off to climax. He comes twice in this sequence. *Manshots* cheered: "Their facial reactions to the flying jism are fun."

Another stellar Yeager scene can be found in "In Your Face," also for Chi Chi, in which the star gets a blowjob from Damien, acknowledged as one of the best cocksuckers in the business.

Contax recalls, "I especially like the 'camera on ground pointing up' view 'cause with Damien doing Ryan we get to see Ryan's curved meat which takes a hard left at about the 5" mark. Straight cocks are nice but curvy ones have so much more personality, don't 'cha think?...At the finish of the video (and I think this is a stroke of genius) director La Rue arranges all nine of his men into a circular daisy chain of biblical proportions. Everyone is sucking someone and being sucked by someone. Then the director tries out his Brian DePalma rotating camera. Standing in the middle of the circle of flesh, he starts turning around and around, cocks and mouths in close-up, faster and faster. I loved the finish. Lots of cum flying through the air. Yeager cums for the third time in the circle. Most of the other guys get a cum shot. No piss elegant queens here. Yeager and Rahm are stand-outs."

About Ryan's appearance in "Powertool 2," Sid Mitchell raved: "Ryan Yeager and Dolph Knight save the day, giving superb performances as an inmate and his visiting lover respectively. Yeager's brilliant performance is not surprise; we've all seen it before. But Knight is a genuine shock, coming across as both convincing and passionate for the first time in his career. It doesn't take much to figure out that Hudson directed the Yeager/Knight scenes, which save the video in spite of itself." If Catalina keeps making jail so attractive, we'll all have to commit a crime just to get in.

Save-the-day Ryan's one of the few who admits to watching his own movies. "It's amazing what they look like after they're done. But getting there is lots of fun. And sometimes, a lot of trouble."

Sometimes fans can be a lot of trouble, too. Ryan says that people don't recognize him but when they do "it's people I don't want to be recognized by."

One of the big dangers in gaymale erotica is overexposure but Ryan says he won't let that happen, carefully picking the roles he wants. And rather than directing, Ryan would like to produce porn, invest in it. "It's always going to be there, there's always going to be a need for it."

Amen.

*

If we love to hate Stryker, then we find stone-faced, disinterested Rex Chandler absolutely disgusting. The scene every fan of erotica awaits is Stryker topping Chandler. Yet this flash-in-the-pan pain in the ass, pun intended, does have his admirers; Joey Stefano said he'd love to make a movie with the star (apparently it's Stefano's goal to be fucked by everybody who is anybody in the business, even a nobody like Chandler).

The aura surrounding blond demi-god Chandler is astounding; because there simply is very little that is sexy about him, it would seem this "act" he's conjured up as the super-straight gives him the appeal he so desperately needs. By refusing to even touch another man's dick he carries the straight man taking his fun where he can get it to its zenith. If he likes pussy so much, why didn't he go into straight porn? The answer is that he could make more money and work fewer hours topping queers. Besides, his girl friend, who often stands alongside on the set to rejuvenate Rex's cock, which often goes limp at the sight of another man naked, might get jealous. One fan summed it up in a letter to *Manshots*: "Rex should put out or stay out."

Before he supposedly retired from the screen, Rex made "Man with the Golden Rod," Marc Fredrics' self-indulgent sequel to the popular "View to a Thrill," and he actually seems to have fun jacking off while two guys go at it on the beach, even going so far as to stick a finger up his ass. He gets to top Dcota and Blade Thompson in what *Manshots* refers to as "his standard metronome fuck." Blade steals the show from Chandler, sucking him with abandon and, as he is being plowed in the missionary position, his meat stays rockhard, and, unlike Rex, he's the kind of star we'll pay to see. And Blade does a sexy rap that Vanilla Ice might well envy, which he wrote himself; is this a David Burrill for the '90s, a singer who also fucks?

Also before his supposed retirement, Rex made Ric Bradshaw's "Rex - Take One," from AVG, about which Sid Mitchell comments: "Fans of Rex Chandler - they must exist somewhere - will be delighted wit this showcase of his 'talents.' And even those of us who are less than enthralled with the blond iceberg will have something to watch in the scenes with the generally fine supporting cast, especially Blade Thompson."

Speaking of icebergs (that just might melt some day), Rex has always maintained that not only can't enjoy sex with men he would absolutely never do it for money. Then one of our spies in Atlanta saw in the local gay publication's classifieds under "Models:" "Rex Chandler - adult film star held over by popular demand. (404) 833-3803. Beeper." Makes you think that perhaps the stud doth protest too much.

*

Long-haired brunet trademeat Steve Ryder was discovered by Chi Chi and put into "In Your Face," released by Catalina. *Contax* described the scene as Ryder peers over a backyard fence in a studio somewhere in Tarzana. "His car has broken down and he's looking for a phone. The guys decide he can use the phone after they use him. That's why it's always good to travel with a cellular phone and an AAA card."

When he moved to Falcon in San Francisco, he became Steven Ryder in "Man Driven," which also featured Matt Gunther and Mark Andrews. Steve, dressed in jockstrap, meets Karl Thomas, dressed in jeans, in a sleazy cross between a bathhouse and a bunkhouse setting and Falcon's publicist described the scene best: "A man with skin tanned golden brown, a muscular body worthy of comparison to the classical Greek statuary of Hercules or Atlas, and a face of such exotic beauty that Karl stopped dead in his tracks and felt his cock bloom into a huge erection." That huge erection was massaged continuously as Karl watched the stud put on a show for him before getting down to the serious business of sucking and fucking, with Thomas bottoming brilliantly (of course, who wouldn't?).

One of Ryder's hottest scenes features a female, in "The Big Switch 3: Bachelor Party," Chi Chi's bisex cipher. *Frontiers'* Rick & Dave described the scene: "Stripper Ryder shows up in a satin-spandex-Phyllis Diller-Chippendales sort of get-up. He strip-dances for her and then she sucks on his dick. She rubs an ice cube all over his dick and butt. Finally he eats her out. We knew that was coming. We wanted to get it over with so we cranked the fast forward button. Tracy sits on him. Steve maintains his erection during the ice cube thing and while she leans over to the nightstand and grabs a glass of water, drinks it and pours it all over him. This guy is some stud keepin' it up with all that cold water! Then he gets on top and this is the first time we have seen the missionary position being done properly." A stud who's been around, obviously.

In "Scoring," the Chi Chi La Rue/Jim Steele co-op effort from Vivid, a star is born. A stud with shoulder length hair. *Frontiers*: "Reviewer Chris loves Steve's Crystal Gayle hair."

Mickey Skee: "Studly Steve Ryder with his gorgeous brown hair..." But Dave Kinnick was gushing about other things: "Steve has a body and face that are so stunning you hardly notice his dick as it waggles past the camera lens in his first scene, a dramatic solo. The scene proves that this is a most beautiful man whom the camera loves like a hot house loves an orchid. His below the-shoulder-length hair so successfully offsets his masculine body and handsome facial features that he comes off less like a mother/daughter act at the Grand Ol'Opry than most of the long-haired boys of porn. In fact, if Steve could play the accordian, he'd be the perfect man. And that's what he must have seemed to Joey Stefano." Stefano's made up his mind to get fucked by every stud in porn heaven and he gets his chance with Steve in "Scoring." Steve is sunning himself on a rock and the scene is photographed in a pool of light from above. As Mickey Skee says, "Stefano shows us what it's like to worship a body from behind, licking the neck, armpit and everything else of the new super-talented Ryder, who everyone is talking about in this video." Sid Mitchell summed it up best: "A brilliantly staged and highly erotic encounter" in which Joey is rewarded for all his licking with a faceful of cum.

But by the time Steve had made "Majestic Knights," featured in a three-way out of what had been a promising duo of Alex Thomas and Danny Summers, it had become what Sid Mitchell described as a definite case of "three's a crowd." All Steve permitted here was to get a blowjob from each of the men. Even Kinnick was hollering: "Come on, Steve, you're in gay porno! Do something gay and pornographic! I think it's very amusing that while Danny Summers is giving him head, Steve cries (at least now he's saying something), 'Oh yeah! Let me come in your mouth!' to which Danny promptly backs off and jacks him, the load falling on Steve's own very nice flat stomach. Next time, Steve, maybe you should say 'please.'"

The occasionally intentionally comic "Majestic Knights" production caused the *Contax* magazine reviewer to call attention to the increasingly alarming post-production snafus caused by directors who care so little about their work they just shoot 'em and forget 'em: "Call it a pet peeve but one of the things that can really ruin a porn flick for me is when the opening credits are inaccurate. Obviously, most viewers of adult material simply fast forward to the first blowjob. I can live with that. But when Steve Ryder is identified as Wes Daniels and Alex Thomas is said to be Steve Ryder and Holly Rider has an 'l' attached to the end of her stage name, it says something bad about post-production and tends to say something bad about the whole production."

The Two Matts...and Tom and Chris

Versatility is what many reviewers scream for. Fans greeted the day Stryker sucked dick with incredible jubilation. They all gasped when he kissed Joey Stefano in "On the Rocks." And we all await the day Jeff takes it up the ass.

But even if he never does do that on screen, at least he's given us a little more than we started with. There are other studs who have romanced the daylights out of their bottoms and even, on occasion, rolled over themselves. No wonder they're superstars.

Take Matt Powers, for instance. (If only we could take him, but he is such an elusive presence, part of his charm.) Now, if a good top these days is hard to find, a good uncut top is even harder to locate. John Holmes was one, but few gay uncuts make it big. But when a cock's built like Matt Powers', well... As Kinnick says: "Matt's cock is of legendary construction: a fat six-inch dick with two somewhat narrower extra inches stuck on at the end at a rakish angle. When erect, it looks like a Concorde jet with its forward fuselage lowered for landing. He seems amiable and kind of shy but performs like a house on fire."

The best of Powers' jabbings are of Vic Summers in "Main Attraction" and Ted Cox in "Lifeguard On Duty." With little Ted hunched over the sofa, Matt rises splendidly to the occasion, causing Ted to come luxuriantly. For the pay-off, practiced Matt lifts Ted up so that the boy is standing up and can explode for the camera, then Matt lets go himself with a gusher across Ted's cute ass. It's a scene so delightful, director Scott Masters has to play it twice in the same video.

*

Another stud who fucks like a house on fire and romances beautifully is Tom Steele, off the screen for a couple of years but back with a vengeance in "All the Way In" and "One Night Stands" (with his singing dubbed by David Burrill, who has a nonsexual - what else? - role in the video) both for Filmco, co-starring with his youthful boyfriend and fellow Texan Scott Jordan, as well as being featured as one of the revellers in "Powertool 2" for Catalina.

Tom's gay and proud of it. As he told me, "I love a big dick in my mouth. Yeah, I like to be top. I love to fuck. I wasn't given this big thing for nothin'. I also love to get sucked. There's nothin' better than a good blow job."

First glimpsed in "Powerline," heavy-lidded, petulant-lipped Tom jacks himself off in fine form early on in the video but when he is surprised by two other guys, he unconvincingly tells them he's straight and what follows is a lacklustre 3-way during which Tom has considerable trouble keeping it up. Hapless Tom watches as one actor goes down on the other. When he is finally semi-erect, Steele enters the scene and the actor starts to suck him. Steele lowers his head and begins sucking the erect nipple of the third guy, but the scene quickly dissolves to a three-way jack off, then more action from the other two, leaving Steele out in the cold. Finally, he sits on the face of the passive guy while he his being fucked and has him lick his balls while Tom jacks off. That's the extent of Steele's appearance, with only minor oral action and no fuck, a terrible waste!

Equally odious was Tom's second outing, "Soldiers," directed by Vincent DePaul and distributed by InHand. Steele got top billing with Neil Thomas in this absurdity which squanders a good plot premise and some decent production values. For the finale, which comes as a blessing after all the limp action which precedes it, Steele and Neil meet each other in the field and Tom "forces" Thomas back to his tent, where Neil tries valiantly to get a rise out of Tom but it's a losing battle. Failing to sustain an erection, Steele drops to his knees in a decidedly un-Stryker pose, to suck Neil's rock-hard dick. Director de Paul must have told Tom he had to fuck somebody so abruptly the scene shifts to that action, the camera showing Steele already in Neil, doggie-style on an army cot, so we are robbed of a view of the entry. The way Neil is cringing, it is obvious Steele's prick is still semi-hard. "Please, make it quick," he groans at one point. Tom told me that he never actually fucked Neil but he did manage to splatter a small dose of juice on Neil's backside. Then it's little trouper Neil's turn to shine as he rolls over on his back and shoots an impressive load. Then, as the final kiss-off, Steele faces the audience, raises a gun, points it into the camera and, smirking, implores us to want him.

Fortunately, good management saved Tom and he appeared in a string of pairings which secured his position. His best partners have included Joey Stefano in "Say Goodbye," Cal Jensen in Matt Sterling's superlative "Heat in the Night," Tim Lowe and Butch Taylor, separately, in Paul Norman's bisexual thriller "Offering," Ryan Edwards (aka Beau Beaumont) and Mark Reardon in "Pledgemasters," and Cal again in "Two Handfuls II" (in a locker room fuck and, later, with Dany Brown), and in a solo, his hard-to-beat jackoff sequence in "Sailor in the Wild II" from Catalina, dressed in cop drag. The best of all remains his pairing with Doug Niles in "Undercover." Talk about fucking!

*

Seeing Matt Gunther in person gives one pause. His sinewy body is even more spectacular than it is on video. His cock is so suckable it is almost obscene. But he is, after all, a performer, and as such, he wears eye makeup, a with-it haircut and clothes that are just so trendy you know he's gay. But the stud obviously loves his work so much you can forgive him anything. Even his sullenness.

That's why the video he did with Jon Vincent, "Inside Jon Vincent," helmed y Chi Chi La Rue, when the tables are decidedly turned, is such a treat. After living through all the scenes in other videos of Matt fucking with such gritty intensity, you can't help but love how Jon must have made him feel with lines like, "On your hands and knees, motherfucker! Get down and suck my cock! I want to pierce that little pink eye of yours." And then when Matt finally gets Jon off, the raunchy one whips Matt's face with his noble prick. What a way to go! With Vincent, Matt of the tight washboard stomach, protruding nipples, and lush cock that tends to bend tantalizingly to the left, gets his ass eaten spectacularly, then gets his ring-equipped cock blown, then fucks his partner doggie-style, only to roll him over and give him a royal screwing that's icing on the cake. In the next sequence, he's attacking big, dirty-tongued Jon Vincent, going down on him with masterful technique as Jon cries, "Let it talk to you baby, let it talk to you." Whatever Jon's cock was saying, Matt must have loved it. Jon says, "Nurse that head baby," and Matt proceeds to do just that, holding Jon back until he can't stand it any more. Matt then goes to Jon's buns, sucking them, slapping them. "I love it," Jon cries, "slap it, baby, slap that ass!" Soon, Jon is so worked up he has to plow Matt's slim ass with his big dick, saying "It's tight, baby." Matt: "Loosen it up. Prong that ass." And does he ever. In another bargain basement production, Stephen Lucas' "Cool Hand Dick," Matt gets blown all the way to his shaved pubes by Sergio Callucci, playing the Spanish warden of a prison in one of our favorite towns, Cornhole, USA. Their opening dialogue is classic:

"What are you in here for, boy?"

"Prostitution, sir."

"And were you good at it?"

"I did what I could, sir."

"You're not like the others here. You've got something more substantial."

And then he proceeds to prove just how substantial Matt is as he blows him, then has him fuck him on top of his desk, sans condom It's a howler of an opening to an otherwise dreadful video.

He can play bottom, as he does most successfully with Jon Vincent and Jeff Stryker, but it's as a true stud Matt stands out, in more ways that one.

Matt was "introduced" by the team of Patrick Dennis in Vivid's "Hole in One," the third in their "Sports" series. Matt's in the shower in the second sequence and in walks, of all people, Joey Stefano, to take a leak. One thing leads to another, as these things have a way of doing, and Joey says, "I hear you're pretty good." Matt: "Why don't you find out for yourself?" And he certainly does. And good is putting it mildly.

Matt also appeared in Patrick Dennis' "First Mate," a decidedly low-budget effort by Vivid standards. The set was a joke, a 30-foot-long crudely painted seascape set behind some sand transported from Malibu. One reviewer said: "The young men manage to have sex with each other in spite of their bewilderment at being placed on this island by incomprehensible forces. The long and deliberate screwing Matt Gunther gives Nick Leonetti, situated as they are on the ground only inches away from the backdrop, wearing passionless looks on their faces, reinforces the abstraction that we are tools of a machine age capable of creating this 'sea.' Leonetti's limp tool is a symbol of our collective impotence when faced with progress. Industry and science are represented by Gunther's erect member." To say nothing of commerce, since these boys were being paid to do this, but, alas, not nearly enough.

Luck was with Matt, though, because a sequence he did with Buck Tanner ended up in Matt Sterling's "Idol Eyes," introducing Ryan Idol. The *Manshots* reviewer: "Gunther deep throats Tanner and like a cat he spasmodically shakes his head from side to side with his prey in his mouth. Later, he licks Tanner's back while fucking him doggie-style. Meanwhile, Tanner's semi-hard cock flips in the air with every thrust he receives."

And Matt loves a crowd, dancing in a club or the sleazy strip joints in New York or doing a video, especially for Falcon. While threatening to become a permanent resident of Falcon's spermbank stock company, Matt appeared in two segments of "Man Driven," a duo, inter-cut with another duo going on at the same bathhouse-style club, an unusual technique for this producer, and then a four way at the end. Two doses of Matt participating with his normal lusty abandon in one video is to OD on the stud. This after "Cruisin' II: Men on the Make," the Falcon release preceding it. In "Cruisin'," Brad Mitchell cries, "Give me your cock!" and that kind of pleading always turns manly Matt on. After giving him a wild probing, he gets Dcota and while Dcota is topping Mitchell, he climbs on and jams his meat into Dcota's butthole for the highlight of the video. His scene at the end with Brad Mitchell pales by comparison.

But the crowd never comes to the party in "The Abduction," where there's a secret hideout with cages, dungeons, blindfolds, handcuffs, dildos, hot wax handy in order to assist the commanders in their lusty interrogations. With the requisite atmosphere set early on, when guards Nick Manetti and Matt start looking for a cozy spot to get it on. They find it in an equipment room where, to the hum of a Trane air compressor, they kiss and in no time Matt's going down on Nick, then gets him down on all fours for a mean fuck.

In their review of this film, *Contax* praised Matt's chest, what he called "the best pair of titties in the business. They're hard, they stand up at attention and they're just perfectly shaped. This is what male boobs are supposed to look like." Then Matt re-appears for a duo but to the video's great discredit, the hoped-for grand finale *ala* "The Other Side of Aspen (I and II)," the producers' classics of this genre, never materializes.

But leave it to Chi Chi La Rue to come up with our favorite Matt Gunther scene, in "Stranded," where he is ravaged by two country studs who pick him up and lay him out in a bar. As Mickey Skee commented, "Matt's spiked short hair and his deep groans are very nice." Mmmmm, are they ever!

Amazingly, Matt can be the fuckee with as much as abandon as he is the fucker, as he proved in "Stranded." After lots of kissing, Matt face fucks his partner and comes in his throat. Then he lets the guy fuck him doggie style:

"You like that don't you," Jason Ross asks, "that fat cock up your ass?"

"Yeah, oh, ah, ah."

"Yeah, there we go, boy."

"Oh, yeah."

"Oh, yeah, there we go, boy."

"Oh," Matt cries, jacking off wildly, "oh, baby, ram that home!" Mmmmm.

*

Jim Steel, one half of the Patrick Dennis team that made so many wonderful videos for Vivid, recalls meeting durable blond topman Chris McKenzie: "He was a brand new face. Never been shot before. At one point, we were both looking at the monitor and the videographer was doing a slow pan down his body and we just looked at each. There was absolutely nothing wrong with that guy's body. I was saying it hit us both at the same time. I think to this day he's incredible."

About Chris' scene in "Superhunks" where he walks around the pool with an erection, Steel remembers, "Some of the hottest moments in video are things like that, that you don't plan. You just get it, and later you realize what you have. A moment like that, you could tell somebody to do it a hundred times and never get it. Chris just did it. I asked him to stand up and walk. I never knew people would go apeshit over it. It's real. It's just real, and the fact that it's real is what makes the scene something that you watch over and over again."

The team used Chris successfully in one of their last efforts together for Vivid, "Between the Sheets," a humorless parody of "How to Marry a Millionaire." *Contax* reported: "McKenzie has starred in several Vivid productions; he's a good looking guy with short blond hair, a decent body and a more than decent pecker. He most always gives his lines a good reading. First Chris gets to fuck twink newcomer Kelly Morgan who unfortunately stays limp throughout and has to have his cum shot faked. This is probably because, earlier, Kelly fucked Craig Slater and came. I mean, the boy was tired! Morgan is a smaller blond with semi-short hair that's had nuclear mouse added to it. (He) ends up looking a bit like a rooster with his 'standing on end' follicles. Even when he takes a dip in the pool later on, that mousse stays in control and his hair looks like he just had it done by Vidal Sassoon. His real problem is that he can't deliver his lines and his accent comes and goes but at least he has a fat cock that comes to an abrupt finish with a pointing head." The production is saved by what Dave Kinnick calls the best scene in the video, Chris fucking Jason Ross. Kinnick says the scene works because of "the exciting contrast of the Nordic and icy and the dark and sensual." *Contax* reported on what happened after the fucking stopped: "The two end up standing side by side and whacking off. Ross never does come but we do get to watch Chris go through the stage of pre-climax where his right tittie keeps flexing up and down, up and down...

"It also demonstrates how important it is to make the audience believe the performers are hot and bothered by it all, that it's the most spontaneous thing in the world to be doing, and so often it's forced and you can tell it is. With Chris and Jason that is excitingly evident, in sharp contrast to his earlier pairing with Morgan."

In "Trading Up," also for Vivid, Chris was, to quote Kinnick, "delightful as (Craig Slater's) current bimbo." And even when mired in such drek as John Summers' "Junior Crew," which Mickey Skee called one of "the silliest videos around," Chris gives his all. As Sid Mitchell commented, "Chris steals the show as the crew captain." A treat for McKenzie fans was his kissing in Jeff Lawrence's otherwise dull "Sizzle," which featured such stellar performers as Dudley the Dog and Sparky O'Toole, about whom Chris has kind words: "He's smarter than people think he is."

When asked who his favorite sex partner was, Chris says: "Lon Flexxe. We got along very well." (Chris and Lon seduced Joey Stefano in the barroom scene in "More of A Man.") And his favorite sex act: "Just call me little oral Annie. And I like it sleazy, but clean. You can act like a slut but when it actually comes down to having sex, you don't have to be all scummy and dirty and covered with lube and spit and shit and stuff like that. You can be very clean about it and still be pretty sleazy."

Okay.

In a Separate Category: Joe Simmons

Quick, name the "quintessential black stud."

It's certainly not pudgy Randy Cochran, who seems to do anything with anybody. But it certainly could be Joe Simmons, who seems not to really want to do anything with anybody, which is the point, after all. If a white guy's going to go this far, well, it has to be this way, going all the way with a living work of art. After all, even Jesse Helms knows *this* work of art, from the late Robert Mapplethorpe's "Black Book," circa 1986, and by his real name, Tom. About photographer Robert, Joe will say only, "Our relationship lasted until his death."

Mapplethorpe said: "At some point I started photographing black men. It was an area that hadn't been explored intensively. If you went through the history of nude male photography, there were very few black subjects. I found that I could take pictures of black men that were so subtle and the form was so photographical." One of his models, Ken Moody, said: "I don't think of it as exploitation. It's almost as if he wants to give a gift to this particular group. He wants to create something very beautiful and give it to them..." And, along with other heroic black studs, Robert gave us Simmons.

When Joe found himself an integral part of the internationally reported flap about the photographic exhibit of Mapplethorpe (several of which featured him), the star spoke out, saying he didn't think that even hard-core porn would hurt people: "People have every right to see it, and the people who don't want it don't have to look at it. And, in that sense, I don't see how it could possibly ever hurt anyone. And if it is hurting someone, they don't have to watch it. I don't think kids can be hurt by it. Our society is -as far as sexuality goes -still a baby. I travel around the world and I find Europeans are so often cool about sexuality, and not only to themselves but to their children. I thought it was wonderful when I walked into a house and I saw a nude man and a picture of a nude female showing genitals and kids running around the apartment. Over there it's a work of art."

Speaking of works of art, Joe's in the gym four days a week, 90 minutes at a stretch. He gets a lot of rest, diets, keeps to a routine. That's how me maintains his 6'3", 190 lb. body. Other statistics: 32" waist, 11 shoe, 44 long suit, 16" neck, 48" chest, and, of course, last but certainly not least, the 9" long cock, hardly Long Dong Silver but prodigious nonetheless.

For the most part, Joe's been used in his 30-odd videos as the stereotypical black stud, which bothers him a bit. "In videos I usually appear, perform sex, then disappear. Very seldom am I a fully realized character with a home, a job, a life." But he doesn't regret the experiences. In fact, they've made him somewhat of an exhibitionist. "I really didn't think I'd go that far, I've always been a shy person. Video has reversed my shyness."

In "Sizzling Joe Simmons," the stud's in control throughout but when it ends, the shy-guy takes over. Suddenly, he's a young man bathed in perspiration, thanking his co-worker. And in Catalina's "South of the Border," (in a review of which Aaron Travis calls him, "Bossman Joe Simmons, a tall, cool drink of chocolate") he turns end-up for Roberto Arias. The video, directed by Chet Thomas, with Orlando Bello on the second camera, drew nearly unanimous praise. About Joe, *Manshots* raved: "Simmons makes a welcome return to the screen after too long an absence. His large, muscular body complements the equally large tool between his legs. His relaxed, easygoing manner suits him well and his bellybutton, an outie, is just beautiful. He goes from straight, pursued trade in his first scene to aggressor and bottom in his last. And it is a sight to see him hunched over a table, getting rammed by the smaller framed, shorter Arias." Fiction mirroring life perhaps? One can only dream. Joe can't remember the name of his favorite co-star but it was the one in "Dirty Tricks."

During the year, Joe appeared in "Black Workout, Part 3," from Filmco, and with an attractive all-black cast, the action is never dull. But the heavy focus is on group sex that left many viewers confused. But Sid Mitchell cheered the star: "Joe Simmons shines as a gym manager distraught by all the hanky-panky he winesses but is unable to resist joining in."

Ah, but it is we who cannot resist. And because we have so few opportunities is part of the charm. "I don't do too many videos because I don't want to get overexposed," he says. We admire the stud's many talents. Being a porn star was not the native New Yorker's original destination: "I studied acting for two years. I've done five Off-Broadway shows, all musicals. I sing. I dance. I play piano and guitar."

And dance he does, in gay and straight clubs. "I don't jackoff in straight clubs. I keep the briefs on for straight performances. It's just erotic dancing. In gay clubs, I do a jackoff scene. I do five shows a day, seven days a week. Every show is not jerkoff, but it's pretty much masturbating, and they're not easy. A lot of people don't realize how difficult it is when you have to do that many shows a day, every week. It takes a strong person to survive it."

His marvelous moves inspired me to use Joe as the basis for my character Snake Russell in my roman a' clef "The Bigger They Are..." (now book one of "Angel: The Complete Quintet").

Like the character in my fictional treatment, when it comes to relationships, Joe considers himself a bisexual: "I had a girlfriend, we broke up, we went back together, we broke up again, she moved back to her country, and after that I started doing gay videos." But gay videos were hardly the beginning of Joe's mansex experiences. His earliest gay encounter was when he was 17: "He was my roommate at the time. I didn't like it at first and afterward we both felt guilty and pretended that it never happened." Later, when he was 22 or 23 (he's 31 now), he had an affair with a man, 42. "He was like a father to me." (Don't you just love it when guys say that?)

"I didn't know what his intentions were," Joe went on about this man. "He used to hug me. I thought it was sensual. And before you know it, there I was, bonded with this guy, having a relationship. But I didn't think for a moment that it was anything involved with being gay. If you are brought up in a sitation where you don't have a father and your mother can't comfort you, well, it feels good having someone hold you. It just kind of grew."

Moral: Never underestimate the power of a hug.

Vince Cobretti

Like bad pennies, hustlers always have a habit of turning up, so it didn't surprise me that shortly after Easter, out of the blue, Vince called one of my associates saying he'd lost my phone number. (I recalled that the last time he was with me he was conducting a desperate, futile search for his appointment book which he had left in a lounge at one of the innumerable airports he was always passing through).

We had kept up with his checkered career, a series of mostly dismal videos for the low-rent end of the business, going for the cheap shot, occasionally hitting it right with such as "Lust Boys" or "Houseboys," but mostly in bilge such as "Hard Moves," during which he can't even keep it up to fuck Joey Stefano. We decided his renewed interest in me at Easter stemmed from his having seen one of the ads promoting the original book about him, "A Charmed Life," although later he told a club owner he found out about it because his sister had walked into a bookstore in Los Angeles and seen it, saying what a coincidence it was there was someone named Vince Cobretti that looked so much like him. I had heard another version of this "Vince's greatest fears" story before, in connection with his porn video career, which was a more plausible scenario since the star has made bisexual videos and his sister could conceivably venture into a video store to rent a tape and there he would be. But it strains credibility to think she'd even find even the bookstores, A Different Light or Circus of Books, the outlets in the city that carry my books, and just by chance spy the book stacked somewhere in the back of the store, most likely in the "Sex" section.

The manner by which the star finally realized, after a year, the book was published didn't really matter. What did matter was his demand to my associate that "it's about time" he start "making some money out of this thing." Little did he know the book had sold out and a new edition with other material was being contemplated.

When he called me, I was out of town and he was forced to leave his number on the machine. Arriving home, I was told that he was coming to Florida and would be dancing at the Carousel Club in Tampa. I juggled schedules to attend.

Normally, three "porn stars" constitute the entertainment fare on Thursday nights but the boys were being held over for a special appearance on Saturday in honor of emcee and gad-about-town transvestite Esme Russell's 30th birthday. There were three "stars" on the bill and because of Vince's last-minute plea to his friend, the club owner Alfredo, one of them had to go, but not entirely, as it turned out. Vince told Al he "usually" got $800 to dance but when the owner balked they ended up agreeing on $100 per show.

When my Tampan friends and I arrived at the club a little after ten, the word was "Vinnie" was coming by limo from Orlando and had left at 9:45. This meant he would miss the first show. This permitted the original threesome to go on as scheduled. The motley crew consisted of Lance, not the uncut blond star of early porn but a true dancer who Esme nonetheless introduced as a "porn star." The dark-haired little trooper knew how to work a crowd and stayed on after the show to work it some more to cadge enough cash to make up for being booted from the second show.

Next up was Alexander Jackson, a short, horse-hung Latin who Esme introduced simply as "Alexander," saying he had appeared in "Manhattan Latins," a bunch of solo spots featuring kids fresh off the streets, and "Latin Fever," scenes from "Boys Behind the Bars," badly re-edited. Hardly the stuff of porn heaven, prompting me to wisecrack to one of my associates, "Old porn performers never die, they just go dancing." Hapless Alexander knew from nothing about dancing and even less about crowd-working, but it hardly mattered; most in the audience were content just to stare in awe at the almost gross appendage barely concealed by a black fabric G-string.

The only true "star" in the firmanent that night turned out to be Cal Thomas of Falcon's "Mission Accomplished." This slim, incredibly hung cutie came on stage in purple, skin-tight sequined leotards and a matching cape, both of which he quickly shed, revealing a black fabric G-string similar to the one Alexander favored, apparently de rigeur wear for horse-hung dancers. Periodically through his dance he exposed the full spectcle of his manhood to Esme, who was standing off to the side studying her lines scrawled on a piece of yellow legal paper, and continued the practice as he pranced about in the audience. At show's end, he mounted the tiny platform at the back of the stage and slyly exposed himself completely, which certainly would have got him busted in the backwater, Bible-thumping venue of Tampa. Cal stayed behind to tell Esme about making his first video, Vivid's "Texas Tales," in which he co-starred with Alexander Jackson. "We were all dancing at a club and somebody said we should do a video and so we went out and did it." As such spontaneous things often do, the end product looks it. Noted critic John Rowberry wrote: "Four dull scenes and the slowest circle jerk in recorded history, all set outdoors."

As part of the gala birthday celebration, Cal called Alexander back on stage and they proceeded to drive Esme wild before our eyes, the Latin crouched at her crotch and Cal lifting her black lace cover-up then working her into a transvestite tizzy from behind.

Before exiting the stage, Esme promised Vince Cobretti was coming. As the dj reigned, Al came by with the kind of look only a disgusted hot-blooded Italian could have, complaining that Vince had indeed arrived, in the promised white stretch limo, but accompanied by five others. The star demanded his guests be admitted compliments of the house. Staring the loss of $17.50 in the face, Al flew into a rage, and rather than see Vince lose his chance to pick up some much-needed cash, the group agreed to pay the cover and were admitted, after which Vince proceeded to the dressing room, which at the Carousel is located across the parking lot, making for messy entrances when it rains.

As Esme came back to the stage, the crew Vince brought with him almost shouted her off the stage with cries of "Vinnie!" But, before long, the jets under the platform on stage were spewing smoke and the dj had Vince's personal track on the system. At last, to the strains of the James Bond theme done as an overture and then "Goldfinger," the star appeared. With his wild black hair clamped into a pony tail and his cheeks even more sunken than before, he barely resembled the young beauty that adorned the boxcover of "Lust Boys," used on the cover of "A Charmed Life." But, as soon as his black cloak was tossed aside and he began his patented acrobatic dancing, I saw the splendid, virtually hairless torso I knew so well had not suffered a bit since the last time I ran my hands over every flawless inch of it.

"He still looks good," my friend shouted over the din. I nodded, suddenly to find the star off the stage and gyrating in front of me, his backside wriggling between my legs. But he didn't linger long, slipping from one set of hands to the next and then back on the stage. He lay on his back on the platform and started to slip off the black pants, cueing a great audience participation gimmick, but Vince knows how to seed the crowd and one of his companions rushed to the stage to remove the garment and his boots. Then, clad only in a black satiny G-string, the star continued his acrobatics and I suddenly found him between my thighs again. I slipped my dollar in the strap just above his crack and he was off without a word. As he danced about the room collecting his tips, it struck me that, unlike some of the other dancers to work this venue, he seldom made eye contact with anyone. It was as if a zombie was high on coke, spinning like a top through the smoky barroom in search of a reason to put himself through this madness and finding it each time someone shoved a bill next to his sweaty skin. Then, it seemed, it was over, and Alexander was back on stage, his weaponry now ensconced in a green pouch that left nothing to the imagination.

Vince, dressed all in black re-appeared, not to work the crowd but to chat with his companions. "I think," I ventured to one of my associates, "it's time for me to make a graceful exit."

"Aren't you going to talk to him?" he asked incredulously.

"He doesn't have anything to say to me I haven't heard before."

As I eased my car out of the parking lot, the white stretch limo was pulling up at the front door to ferry Vince and his friends into the night. And, at that moment, I remembered Vince, like all sexualists, alchemizes by moonlight, and sometime, perhaps sooner than later, when the full moon rolls out again and the waves are lapping against the shore just yards from the house, I would be in bed thinking about my lips touching his during the ritual of sex and the whisper that begged for an embrace and I'll be glad, glad for the precious memories.

Chi Chi and His Boys: Damien, Johnny, Jason, and Chad

It seems with some videos, Chi Chi La Rue (aka Taylor Hudson) sets porn back for decades, foregoing attention to detail, then he comes up with a goody such as "Read My Lips." (But even that feature came in for criticism in some quarters, with Mark Glascock of *Southern Exposure* offering this sage advice: "It represents growth for (the) multi-talented director but I like my men, not my movies, uncut. Edit, Chi Chi.")

Chi Chi's alliances with other talented people such as Jerry Douglas (the result being "More Than A Man") or with Vivid on "Davey and the Cruisers," or with Scott Masters at Catalina have helped their product. Chi Chi's help to Masters' product in particular has been notable. He has been able to assist that director in occasionally breaking out of his stagnant formula. Kinnick comments: "...The way of Masters: There are two minutes of flirtation between the two boys, followed by three minutes of A sucking B, then three minutes of B sucking A. Forty-five seconds of anal foreplay cuts directly to A fucking B (joined in progress). At plus 13, B ejaculates, photographed from two angles and connected by a facial close-up. Thirty seconds later, A comes, and the post-sex dialogue establishes why they won't see each other again. If you don't mind seeing the same sights every time you travel down a particular highway, you'll really like this stretch of road, if only for it being so easy on the eyes." To say nothing of the brain. And when left unattended, Masters and his cinematographer Josh Eliot commit the unpardonable sin of not permitting us to share the orgasm of the man who is cumming. This is a pet peeve of *Frontiers*: "Would you porn guys please pull your cameras back during those cum shots? We want to see the faces of the dudes as they are having their orgasms. We like to see them tossing their heads back, squeezing their eyes shut, thrusting their hips, muttering nasty words as they shoot off. It's not enough just to see a dick squirting. We want more. If you feel like you have to use an extreme close-up, get an extra camera just for that. And if the guys are too ugly to show their faces, then get other guys."

Shooting an orgasm is something Chi Chi normally doesn't have a problem with. And there's no particular pattern, except to showcase his own star discoveries in the best possible light.

Ryan Yeager and Steve Ryder are only a couple of many who extol Chi Chi's virtues. And when Tony Davis brought Joey Stefano to Hollywood, he knew Chi Chi would know what to do with the now infamous, self-proclaimed "sex maniac."

The La Rue stable currently boasts the workhorses of the industry who, unlike Ryan Yeager, don't mind being overexposed.

Chief among the denizens is Damien, whom Mickey Skee describes as "the primo buffed-out model with an angular face, olive-colored skin with long black hair that occasionally flops in his face." The boy's hair has gotten him much press. In its review of "Sex Bi Flex," *Contax* magazine says, "Damien's hair has gotten totally out of control. It's luxuriously full and has a Laura Petrie/Marilyn Quayle flip on the sides. Damien should get a contract with a hair care company. His hair pees!"

Later, when Damien made "Majestic Knights" for Paul Norman's company, with Sebastian Lore directing, the *Contax* reviewer was at last satisfied: "He's finally gotten his hair under control. The ponytail is gone and even the big clump of hair above his forehead has been trimmed. He's finally graduated from Super Cuts to a barber and the result is that it's now possible to look at him without being distracted by his hair. And looking at Damien is always a treat."

A treat, too, is the fact that sex-crazed Damien has followed Joey Stefano's example of lapping up his own cum, most notably in Scott Masters' "Master Piece." But scene-stealing has become de rigeur for Damien. In his review of Vivid's "Summertime Blues," Kinnick comments, "Damien definitely steals this otherwise mediocre video. In just a few short months, he has become the premiere sister/father confessor/girlfriend/stud/everyman in the gay video industry. Not only is he La Rue's right arm these days, but he's a versatile, outgoing sexual dynamo in his own right. When he's not topping one of the top stars of the industry, he's bottoming with the best. When he's not sexing, he's doing the sexers' make-up, he's off setting a fashion trend somewhere."

As far as sexing goes, Damien has a talent for rimming. Says Kinnick of Damien's working over of Austin Moore in "Blues:" "He tongues butt with the precision that a Swiss watchmaker reserves for a top-of-the-line Rolex. Austin makes mewing noises and funny faces as Damien sticks first his tongue, then his finger, then globs of spit, then finally his rubber-covered pony into the upturned buttocks."

Newcomer Robbie Swenson stole Damien's starring vehicle "The Boy Next Door," for Vivid, directed by Jim Steel, also featuring Johnny Rahm, in his fuck with Todd Fuller in a shower and the adjacent bathtub. Damien's next outing for the same studio and director, "Truth, Dare or Damien," was another loser, highlighted only by his fuck with Danny Summers. Regarding the boxcover, Sid Mitchell comments: "Packaging will not appeal to most gay viewers; Damien is air-brushed into nonentity."

Yet, airbrush or no airbrush, it's hard to imagine Damien ever being a nonentity.

Another darkly handsome La Rue stableboy is the aptly named, nicely long-penised Johnny Rahm, a kid who has been ramming it all over the place lately.

Traditionally a bottom, he proved his versatility in "Trading Up" from the Patrick Dennis team at Vivid. And, boy, was he surprised that tradelike Scott Martin (who looks like Gary Grimes of the wonderful film "Summer of 42" as a grownup) could take all that luxurious lean meat down his throat. So invigorating was this blowjob that *Contax's* reviewer said, "Martin is sucking on Johnny's hardon and it begins to sound like a Banshee is at the window. Lighten up Johnny, just lie there and enjoy yourself but shut up already. Rahm almost knocks over a huge cactus on the nightstand (ouch!), then leans over and attacks Scott's cock, which I would have done long ago were I in a similar position. Rahm then repositions himself so he's lying on his back with his head in the pillow. Scott straddles him and fucks what he calls 'his mouth pussy.' With a Prince poster on the wall looking down on the guys, Rahm fucks Scott, which is totally unexpected because most of the time the big guy is on top of the little guy. Scott never removes his sneakers for the various positions he's fucked in, perhaps in silent protest to being made to bottom. Later, Scott bottoms again and I guess that must mean he's found his niche."

Sid Mitchell raved about brooding, brown-eyed Rahm: "The best performance is from newcomer Johnny Rahm, who in spite of his total irrelevance to the main plot, steals the show hands down, no contest. Here is a star already at home with dialogue, flashing a ball-busting smile, and boasting a sense of timing that would make a stand-up comic proud. If he had been given the lead instead of Martin, the mind boggles at what might have been." Sid also commented about the absurd packaging, featuring Scott wearing more lipstick than Marilyn Monroe or David Bowie. Also for Vivid, Johnny appears with Todd Fuller in "The Boy Next Door," as well as "Jackhammer" and "Movers and Shakers."

And then it was on to San Francisco for the so-called "super-dicked" star as coverboy (with that dick leaning entincingly to the left) for Falcon/Jocks' "The First Time," playing a cultural illiterate who's never seen a gay porn magazine. David Grant plays the guy who introduces him to such uplifting pleasures and before you know it Rahm's squatting on David's meat for a beautifully filmed screwing. But one can only imagine what fun they could have had afterward if Rahm had said, "Hey, I've got a surprise for you!" and played David one of his videos! Unfortunately, Johnny didn't stick around to add some zest to the three way at the end featuring David and Trevor Hansen and Eric Rieger. Jocks also inserted him, in more ways than one, in "On the Lookout" in which he was lustily topped by Bill Carson, a black stud with an awesomely long and fat endowment, while sucking Rob Decker.

Never one to sit still for long, Johnny popped up in the quickies "Sex Bazaar Pt. 2," "Oral Report" (also starring Vince Cobretti) and "Exiled!" out of the low-end mail-order video specialists, Club M Studios, and for Toby Ross in "Once in a Blue Moon," making whoopee with Marcus Braun, switching roles. It was in this film (as "Jonnie Rohm") that he got raves from *Manshots*: "Ross' camera has to race to keep up with these two. Special note should be made of Rohm, whose dark good looks are complemented by a long, curved, photogenic cock and who provides an impressive money shot." And that's where the money's at, as the saying goes.

Johnny's always impressive money shots made it into Filmco's "All the Way In," which is stolen by a young find named Scott Jordan, boyfriend of star Tom Steel, and scores mightily in "The Devil and Danny Webster" for Richard Lawrence, wherein he gets a royal fucking from Jason Ross (which includes the immortal line, recited by Ross while sucking the Rahm cock, "Goes around corners, eh?") and gets to lay it into longhaired blond Tommy Wilde after enjoying a laborious blowjob.

But it is for Chi Chi that Johnny seems to shine brightest. Even in otherwise dismal surroundings, Johnny's turns in the all-oral "In Your Face" and "Big Switch 3: The Bachelor Party" are stellar. Also at Catalina, Johnny appeared for Scott Masters in "Master Piece," with Scott Martin, and "Man of the Year," trying to be what Mickey Skee calls "a rough guy on a motorcyle" and does a scene in a mirror that "makes him look a lot like Keanu Reeves."

Meanwhile, Johnny and his ever-hard cock were toiling in the lowrent videos of Gino Colbert, beginning with "Boxer II" with Chris Stone, Vladimir Correa, and Rod Garretto, then "Brotherly Love II," featuring the mind boggling spectacle of blond (and nationally advertised bisexual) Marc Radcliffe (whom Chris McKenzie can't even remember appearing with, and no wonder) and Indian-blooded Johnny as brothers, then what we had thought was the worst of the bunch, "Manhandler," until "Boys Will Be

Boys" showed up. As *Frontiers* reported, "Welcome to the new world order! Of course it's all run by queens (not the Elizabethan kind). We have two (or maybe more) fictional governments in a cold war setting and lots of gayboys putting on accents they have no business attempting. It centers around an Arab prince and his mommy's crown jewels." At least Johnny's crown jewels glittered amid this spectacle. Cheered *Frontiers*: "What we enjoyed most about this flick was Johnny Rahm. With Johnny, even routine sex scenes can make us sweat." And despite such incredible overexposure in some of the worst videos of all time, as long as Johnny can continue to make people sweat, and cum on cue, he'll continue to find work.

*

Jason Ross is another one of those performers who is everywhere, working for anyone in anything, a versatile utility infielder for the '90s, a kid who can top as well as bottom. He's so good he was voted "Best Newcomer of the Year" in 1991 by *Adult Video News*.

We first noticed the hunk that Mickey Skee calls "a Robert Downey Jr. lookalike, ever-cute, with that dimpled chin," in John Travis' "Hard Steal," being expertly rimmed by (and later topped by) John Clayton. Then he popped up in "Tattoo Love Boy," another inept entry from InHand, directed by Chi Chi La Rue and starring heavily tattooed pool boy Marc Anthony, a street-trashy, muscular dude who appears to have dropped out of an Old Reliable flick, a marked departure in casting for the normally chichi director. Jason gets his chance with the hunk at the end of the flick in a four way. *Manshots* said of Jason at the time, "he's quickly rising to the ranks of stardom."

Quickly rising being the name of the game, Jason has enhanced his reputation by suviving insipid videos and doing it with panache. He has demonstrated a great skill for cocksucking, for instance. In "Behind the Eight Ball," from Vivid, directed by the now defunct team of Patrick & Dennis, the star offers a realistic blowjob, replete with gagging and choking, and a wild doggie-fuck by redheaded Troy Neilson, then mounting him for a wild ride in the saddle. "Ross is always a delight to see," *Manshots* was now raving.

Also for the studio, Jason joined the new and the old Vivid faces in "Hot Summer Knights," the cast including Jason Cruise and Scott Hogan, "Club Men," and he was the coverboy on Jim Steel's "Bedroom Eyes," wherein his reading of a book, "How to Become a Male Sex Symbol," is the link for the episodes. Dave Kinnick: "Get this: A lesson on the anatomy of a sexless sex film; an amusing little story with nothing to flesh it out, so to speak. Jason Ross gives a nice performance as the boy who's never gotten any but is convinced he's gonna get it by mastering the secrets (in the book). What he doesn't get is the fact that he already has a a perfect set of squintees that have melted the hearts of everyone around him." Unfortunately, the cast seldom clicks when it comes to sex and this one misses the mark by a mile. Steel, indicted during the year for directing a video that was judged obscene in Oklahoma, must wonder: Are things like this worth going to jail for?

For Filmco, in the otherwise dismal "One Night Stands," starring that great nonperformer David Burrill, Jason plays a junkie with finesse, getting it on with his dealer before he very believably succumbs to an overdose.

At VCA/HIS, Ross was unquestionably the star of "Callguys USA," a Garth Evans effort. The trite storyline revolved around him as a Beverly Hills pimp. At first, we see him poolside fantasizing about Buck Tanner and, talk about the unexpected, the salacious bottom tops the hunk. Coming out of his fantasy, he rams himself with a dildo. Even that doesn't cut it and next we see him masturbating while he's taking a call on his cellular phone, a call from his manservant (Scott Martin) telling him a boy has come for an interview. One thing leads to another and Jason regales his new recruit with stories (that we see as hardcore vignettes) about just what it takes to be an escort. At the finale, the manservant enters the scene to plug Jason, giving what the one reviewer called, "a whole new meaning to the word 'manservant.'" Sid Mitchell raved: "Jason Ross makes a delightfully uninhibited, even sleazy 'madam' in spite of the all-too-familiar lines he is asked to deliver."

Frontiers also applauded the performance Ross gave in "Headstruck" another Chi Chi La Rue elixir from Catalina with the premise, "What if you could convince your hunky straight roommate that he's gay?" "We start with Ryan Yeager and Jason Ross who look like they just got back from shopping on Melrose. A recycled Costello Presley tune assaults our ears. They go inside Jason's apartment and start kissing. They have very sexy stubble on their faces, but is it real stubble or 'Gender' stubble? Suddenly, they are soaking and sucking in the tub. Jason Ross looks very good wet...The finale is watching these studs put their clothes back on afterward. (It's hotter than it sounds.)" Tony Erickson (aka Sinatra) plays Jason's roommate who catches them together and is nonplussed. Then he falls on the stairs and gets amnesia. Eventually the lad figures out that what he needs is a cock in his mouth to job his memory, but when Jason sees the Erickson erection he just can't wait to get it in his own mouth. *Manshots* raved that Ross "spectacularly deep-throats Yeager, and later, in a film rarity, jacks him off to climax. Their facial reactions to the flying jism are fun." Yeager was so turned on he came twice in this sequence. Ross seems to have that effect on guys.

Ross often gets stuck in claptrap such as "Hawaiian Desire," also by Garth Evans, who has a penchant for wrapping touristy footage around drab bedroom action. Dave Kinnick bemoans the fact that in this case, "even Jason Ross has trouble and is half-limp when he comes as Zeff Ryan fucks him. Maybe the music is a contributing factor since it sounds like Barry Manilow on the wrong drugs."

In Vivid's "Between the Sheets" Jason gets together with another great hugger and kisser, Chris McKenzie. *Contax* magazine described what came after the foreplay: "When they get around to fucking it's Chris fucking Ross. Their second position has Ross leaning into a mirrored wall with Chris plowing him from behind. At one point, though, Ross rears back and sprays his mirror image with spit. Chris just pushes Jason into the mirror and grinds the side of his face in the dripping spit. Weird!"

In Falcon's "The Big Ones," Jason tops Scott Hogan after Scott's been plowed by Alex Thomas and the second time does the trick, while Ross is pulling his head back by a hank of hair, Thomas comes and Ross yells "Whoa!"

Perhaps someone should say that to Jason, Whoa! Enough already. Slow down, kid, there's plenty of time.

*

There are so many Knights around you need a scorecard. There's Kevin Knight, Ryan Knight and Dolph Knight and god-knows-who-all and videos called "Knights of Thunder" and "Hot Summer Knights," but there is only one Chad Knight, and he even has to his credit his own vehicle, Stryker-style, "Knight Moves." With this one, Jim Steel's first solo effort from Vivid after the breakup of the "Patrick Dennis" team, Jim proved he could do it alone, with some help from Chad. At the time of the video's release, Sid Mitchell lauded Chad's performance, saying that he gave "undoubtedly the most erotic and most charming performance of his career," saving this otherwise inept video from oblivion with its bad camera work, repetitive music and unfulfilled ideas. Vivid's stable of performers assisted, including Scott Hogan and Grant Fagin, the boy who loves to suck his own dick.

We first noticed Chad in "Someone's Watching," out of the Jocks/Falcon machine, one of his best features over-all. Sid Mitchell called it "one of the most imaginative, delightful features of the year," the only complaints being the ones usually associated with all Falcon productions, that the people responsible behind the camera are never identified and the running time is barely an hour. They manage to advertise 90 minutes because they tack on interminable previews. Besides Chad, the film boasts Trevor Hansen as a masculine guy with a pleasantly gay attitude, for a change.

After seeing Chad's next, "Compulsion - He's Gotta Have It," which he made for Falcon (Pac #72), *Contax* magazine's reviewer was in awe: "Chad Knight is God! There, I've said it. I've said it and there's been no thunder clap in the distance so I guess it's got to be true. Chad Knight is God! I last spotted Chad in 'Someone's Watching' and I suppose at the time I had mistaken that little stud-puppy Jim Montana for God so all I remember about Chad was that he could stand a few extra pounds on those ribs. Strange how these things work. Back then, Montana was god, and now it's Chad Knight. The only way I can possibly make amends to God Chad is to gush about him whenever I mention his name." In this video, Scott Hogan gets to lay it into Chad, beginning in a pool. "In a flash he's in Chad's craving love hole (excuse me, I just had to use that one this time.) Scott fucks like a pro, really giving it to Chad who eggs him on with loud moans and words that effect." Noticing neighbor Trevor Hansen watching them, the boys get into numerous positions, the last one being Chad on his hands and knees with a sloped back and his ass high in the air. *Contax* sums up: "Chad deserves sex-kitten status the same as I once conferred on Joey Stefano."

By the time Chad made "Knight Moves" for Vivid, he'd slipped a notch in *Contax* estimation, from God to Prince: "My but what a difference a few ounces of Clairol can make! Chad didn't go totally weird with his hair so he's still okay in my book. He let it go natural (brown) and got it buzzed on the sides real short. Then with what he left on top he squared it off, flat-top style, and put enough Dippity-Doo in it to hold it stiff and spiny in a Force-4 hurricane. But that's okay. He's a twink, and twinks can get away with almost any eccentric type hairdoo." Especially when they're sex kittens.

And this kitten is just as good at giving it as he is taking it, as evidenced in "Score Ten," in his scene with Blade Thompson, wherein Chad starts by breaking into lockers and sniffing jock-straps. Kinnick: "A scene the whole production should strive to live up to...They perform in an extended duo that is perfectly acted by both men. Chad is the locker room tourist who wants to put his dick up a jock's ass just once. In order to obtain his goal, he first gives Blade a nice handjob, resulting in a fist full of come, then bends over and takes Blade's still hard (and rubber sheathed) cock up his butt. Following this, there is some really nice dialogue and a big switch, as Blade softens and plays bottom for the determined boy. After the fourth nice wet shot in the scene, it ends with a really great hug."

Versatile Chad can also perform with a female slut, as evidenced in "Big Switch 3, Bachelor Party," from Catalina, a party to which director La Rue also invited Johnny Rahm, Steve Ryder, and Mark Andrews. In both scenes 1 and 3, Chad's ass takes over for the girl's pussy halfway through the scene and the poor kid has to lick twat while taking the pounding behind.

This video was the perfect example of how restricted budgets have come upon the house of Higgins (William). It used to be Catalina specialized in realistic interior seetings and occasionally, when appropriate, spectacular scenery to spice up the goings-on. "Pacific Coast Highway," "Sailor in the Wild," ad nauseum, set the tone for the sex romps to follow. Now it seems that La Rue has taken over, along with Scott Masters and Josh Eliot, and that means no locations and tacky sets. No self-respecting set designer could have lent his name to the dismal settings in "The Big Switch 3: Bachelor Party." The only sequence that works is Steve Ryder as a private dancer, and that same set is recycled in "Sex Bi Flex," with anti-hero Lex Baldwin. Talk about tacky.

Also at Catalina, snaggle-toothed Chad labored in "Pacific Coast Highway II" (in which he shares a three-way with Craig Slater and Kyle Roman) and appeared under Scott Masters' direction toiling in the equally awful "Bedtime Stories" and "Loaded." (Danny Summers, however, stole the show in the former, one of the few of Masters' works not filmed by Josh Eliot.) Also for Catalina, Chad showed remarkable acting ability in "Spellbound for Action," another Scott Masters production, this time directed by Chet Thomas. As reported by Mickey Skee: "He starts out as a nerd and find a Love Potion #9 which turns him into a stud with a nine-and-a half inch dick...Chad has a wicked innocence and a killer body with a perky dick that pokes straight up to his belly button."

The perky pecker gets a real workout in the Jim Steele/Chi Chi La Rue effort "Scoring," when the now platinum blond gets it on with Damien in front of a seamless black backdrop, and it's sex the way it was meant to be in these fantasies. As Kinnick reports, "A pairing of Damien and Chad Knight sizzles, with Damien delivering a rim job like a Ferrari riding the rail through a carwash. He attacks Chad's butt hole with quick jabs of his tongue, tugs with his fingertips, and delivers small drenchings of well aimed spit. Chad, of course, smiles sweetly. When Damien is done, he pops a load right on Chad's upturned butt hole,. Then before you can say 'hoover,' he's down on his knees licking up his spunk while Chad shoots on or about his own chin."

Talk about perky peckers!

Newcomers of the Year

Billy Houston

Billy Houston is fresh.

And when he smiles he has the cutest dimples around. In fact, this stud puppy is downright adorable, as he realizes at one point in "The Devil and Danny Webster" directed by Richard Lawrence by way of Larry Bronco and YMAC, when he gushes, "I'm gorgeous."

And many videophiles are agreeing, including some who normally go in only for the he-man stud types.

At the beginning of "The Devil and Danny Webster," based on the "Faust"-idea of making a deal with the evil one from down under, Billy Houston plays Danny as a comical nerd, wearing glasses and slumping when he walks. He spends his days spying on his sexy neighbors and his nights watching porn videos. But while he's watching "Damn Yankees" he falls asleep and, alas, the devil comes to Danny and transforms him into what he himself is able to call "gorgeous." "Although we'd take him either way," Kinnick observes, "the transformation seems to inspire Danny and it does give him enough nerve to make a pass at Satan and promptly ball with him." As Zeff Ryan, portraying the devil, is going down on him, Billy sighs, "Oh, Satan gives a helluva blow job." The devil gives Danny two hours to think about the deal, to try it out, leading to an encounter with Jason Ross, whom he fucks in workmanlike fashion, then observes Johnny Rahm and Tommy Wilde in heat. But the hoped for happy ending with Rahm, a duo that would have been hot, never materializes and so the film just fizzles.

But what endeared this vehicle to us was the outtakes tacked on at the end. They show Billy is really enjoying this caper. After seeing this, nobody can say this little boy was "sold into slavery" by some slimeball porn producer. Indeed, Houston, whom the *Manshots* reviewer called "a boyish-bodied, baby faced little brother type," makes the whole thing worthwhile. "He has a beguiling screen presence, a natural ability with dialogue and an apparent spontaneity that makes his explicit scenes charming, even though he's not mega-hung or frenetically energetic. He seems to be a natural sexualist, eager to please and exuding a vulnerability and warmth that are irresistible. He sucks and fucks with an instinctual delight. But it is his aura of innocence that will make him a star if he so chooses."

Billy's follow-up video is "Head Bangers," which has him fucking Wilde at the finale, but most of the screen time he spends popping in on others having sex. In the finale, as Dave Kinnick observes, Tommy's dick "seems to positively shrink whenever a dick goes near his butt, but he hangs in there." Kinnick called the video "an often hot trip to a world that is a hairdresser's nightmare and one of the best youth-oriented titles of the year." One can only hope that under Richard Lawrence's guidance, Billy can let himself be versatile and become the first superstar in the youth category for the '90s.

Danny Summers

Someone has to bottom for all these tops and one of the most serviceable around is Danny Summers (aka Somers in some venues), the Dany Brown of the '90s, whom the Falcon publicist described as "a muscled young jock with a steely sexy look." Summers was featured in the studio's "Man Driven," the willing bottom in the four-way at the end with Matt Gunther, Mark Andrews and Brad Mitchell. For the Jocks division, Danny provided the receptacle for Damien in the first sequence of "Rimshot." This time Falcon's ad copy referred to his "winning smile" and "granite-like physique," then went on to perform the same duty for mustachioed Glenn Steers and at one point cries, "Yeah, I need daddy's dick!" and you just know he does.

But wait, in Jocks/Falcon's "On the Lookout," the tattooed Danny gets to plug Marc Saber with what Falcon calls "superhuman ferocity" (probably because he's had to bottom for so long) and then dark-haired Brad Chase (so cute in "Summertime Blues") in what Falcon called a "primal fucking" that sent these two studs in "sexual orbit," apparently a place where "superhumans" rotate.

Danny was featured in Catalina's "Loaded," "Powertool II," and "Sex in Tight Places," which marked the return of Doug Niles, and for AVG in "How Big Is Danny?" directed by John Summers. Said

Mickey Skee: "It makes a great boxcover but it should be how big can Danny take it? Because that's what happens when chiropractor Danny is working late one night and cleaning man Rod Garetto gets carried away with himself." With an ass as accommodating as Danny's around, who wouldn't?

Book III.
The Best of the Best

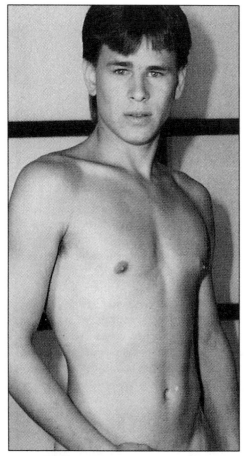

Billy Houston, Newest Young Male Superstar

"The worst thing is a heterosexual film where everyone's looking at their watch. There's joy in gay movies. They have all those flat stomachs and big dicks. It's dirty. There's passion..."

- Al Goldstein, publisher of Screw

The Best of the Best

"While heterosexual characters in art are routinely presented in a balanced way," the late, esteemed film critic and historian Vito Russo wrote, "this has never been true of gays. Gays have an unbroken tradition of being played as either buffoons or villains." Or victims.

But in some films it really doesn't matter how gaymales are treated, they still fascinate, entertain, and illuminate.

The All-Time Best Gay-Themed Films

(Listed Alphabetically)

"Apartment Zero"
This 1989 Hitchcockian psycho-sexual suspense thriller starred Colin Firth (so beautiful in "Another Country") as a nervous closet case and Hart Bochner, who never looked sexier, as a man who rents a room from him. The film is filled with rich and macabre humor.

"The Boys in the Band"
This film version of the long-running play was released in 1970, just after Stonewall, and the entire original cast was kept intact with performances that couldn't be sharper. The more things change, the more they stay the same: the lines and situations are as true today as they were two decades ago.

"The Comfort of Strangers"
Paul Schrader's film about psychosexual hijinks in Venice, magnificently photographed and starring Rupert Everett and Christopher Walken. Lots of Rupert's skin makes this an event, as well as one of the greatest queries in moviedom, from Rupert to his lover Natasha Richardson while he's fucking her: "What does it feel like, being a woman?"

"Death in Venice"
Dirk Bogarde played, with great restraint, an aging bisexual who develops an uncontrollable passion for a young boy (blond Bjorn Andressen) in this superb 1971 Italian production of Thomas Mann's classic, richly textured novella.

"Everlasting Secret Family"
Made in 1989 and recently released on video, this wonderful, razor-sharp Australian production explores the possibilities if the government were controlled by a secret gay society. Mark Lee (Mel Gibson's cute young pal in "Gallipoli") is a strikingly handsome 16-year-old when the movie opens, learning to spread his asscheeks for a married senator. Later, the kid decides to subvert the process to gain some power of his own and therein lies the rub. Bob Satuloff raved: "At a time when gay film is fixated on political and health issues, it's a particular pleasure to see a movie as fascinating, perversely funny and socially dangerous as this."

"La Cage Aux Folles"
This hilarious 1979 comedy became the biggest grossing foreign film ever released in the U.S. *The New Yorker* raved: "...a funny, touching fable of monogamy and personal liberation. This is still one of the few mainstream films in which gays are, in every sense, gay." The sequel, "II," is now also available on video and, although not as refreshing as the original, it nonetheless provides two hours of hilarious fun.

"Law of Desire"
Kevin Thomas of the *L.A. Times* said of Spanish director Pedro Almodovar, "The Fassbinder for the 80's...has the same daring, virtuoso command of the medium." The opening scene in this upside-down, inside-out cornucopia of love in all its guises is brilliant and things just keep swirling around a movie director with two lovers. This absorbing examination of the attractions of absolute desire was suitably praised as "lushly erotic!" by the *Village Voice.*

"Longtime Companion"

This thoughtful 1990 movie originally made for TV won the Triumph of the Human Spirit Award for its depiction of "people overcoming adversity by pulling the best that is in them" and the Psychodramatic Realism Award for its accurate and sensitive portrayal of "individuals dealing with a life crisis." Key to this assessment was Bruce Davison's magnificent performance, especially the scene at the deathbed of his lover, played by Mark Lamos. Having nursed his companion for months, Bruce's character understands he pain and softly, slowly, gently, he talks him into letting go of life. It's a moment to be cherished.

"Maurice"

E. M. Forster's long self-suppressed, posthumously published novel about the platonic relationship of two students was an indictment of homophobia and it was lovingly brought to the screen in 1987 by director James Ivory and senstitively acted by a cast that includes James Wilby and Rupert Graves.

"Midnight Cowboy"

Although not as affecting as it was when it was first released, this, the only X-rated film ever to win the Academy Award as Best Picture (in 1970), remains a vivid portrait of a straight hustler who ends up going with gays to stay alive. Jon Voight is perfect in the title role, ably assisted by Dustin Hoffman as a sleazeball he meets in his travels. Voight's nude from the rear in two scenes, normally scissored when shown on TV.

"My Beautiful Launderette"

"A juicily entertaining movie," said *New York Magazine*. "Stephen Frears directs with an appropriately raw visual palette." London playwright Hanif Kureishi created a marvelous story about Omar, a young Pakistani settled in England, and his affair with Johnny, a street tough. The lovers cross racial and class barriers but it hardly qualifies as a depiction of a gay utopia in this exquisite 1985 film.

"Prick Up Your Ears"

The life of British playwright Joe Orton and his lover, Kenneth Halliwell, is a tragic one, making a sensational book and providing the basis of this superb 1987 film adaptation which boasts Vanessa Redgrave as Joe's agent and expert turns by Gary Oldman and Alfred Molina as the lovers.

"Something For Everyone"

Long before there was the bisexual genre of porn, there was this, Harold Prince's sumptuous 1970 film about an opportunist who manages to charm his way into everyone's heart and bedroom. Doug Richards said: "The camera's focus alternates between the gorgeous scenery and equally gorgeous Michael York. Never has a man been more provocatively lensed outside of hardcore gay porn."

"Sunday Bloody Sunday"

Bisexuality was further explored a year later in this stunning film, again from John Schlesinger with a cast headed by Peter Finch and Glenda Jackson, who share the charms of Murray Head.

"Torch Song Trilogy"

In a class by itself, this hit Broadway play by Harvey Fierstein was transformed into a continually absorbing 1988 movie, a must for Matthew Broderick fans. Said Matthew about his famous love scene: "I slip off to a barn with Ed, Arnold's ex-boyfriend, and we sleep together. And you try to think, 'This is the character.' Brian Kerwin (who plays Ed) seemed to be pretty calm. It took two takes. You know, I can sit here and say that as an actor, you just translate it, it's the same as a heterosexual relationship. But that scene was different...I enjoyed it. It was fun to be romantic, to be sexy with a man. It was so strange, but that I enjoyed. It's a good scene."

"Victim"

This superb 1962 English film starred Dirk Bogarde as a barrister who attempts to quash a blackmail attempt. Doug Richards, writing in *Manshots*: "No one will ever be able to measure the contribution of this movie to the cause (of legalizing homosexuality between consenting adults in private), but it certainly brought the matter before the public and then dramatized it as only an entertaining film can."

"Victor, Victoria"
Robert Preston's performance as a drag queen in this delightful 1982 Blake Edwards spoof is such a gem you never tire of seeing it. Julie Andrews was never more delicious.

The Best Erotic Videos and Scenes

Despite the pleasure they afford, sexual practices are frequently banal, impoverished and doomed to repetition. Erotic scenes must be shot sparingly, with a good deal of economy. The best directors know this, scouring the carnal operation of its tedium and effort. The best scenes have a preparation, a cruising, an approach, perhaps conversation, then the love scene. And I do mean, love scene. Two young men do not know each other but they know they are about to become partners in a specific act, or acts, and they are being paid to put on a performance. What ignites the imagination is the passion they put into it even though they are being paid for it. That is what separates the stars from the has-beens, the best videos from the sludge.

And a bigger budget doesn't always make it either. As Bob Satuloff observes, "Maybe I'm unrepresentative of the audience for gay porn but I keep finding that the slicker a video is - the higher the level of production values, the fancier the camera work, the more scoring, the more gleamingly gym-bodied the performers - the less I seem to like it, or, to put it more succinctly, the less I'm able to use it. In terms of accessibility, the state of the art stuff I've seen lately puts a thick glass wall between me and what I'm watching. It's sufficient unto itself, like a sitcom with a laugh track that provides its own responses; it doesn't need me. On the other hand, gay sex videos that are technologically more primitive, fuzzier, less choreographed, more improvisational and documentary-like - in that the camera is recording whatever it happens to see in a manner that appears almost random - exert a more powerful tidal pull on the part of me that responds to this kind of entertainment."

Perhaps it's passion Bob's missing. As Al Goldstein, publisher of *Screw*, the New York sex newspaper and an acknowledged bisexual, explains: "The worst thing is a heterosexual film where everyone's looking at their watch. There's joy in gay movies. They have all those flat stomachs and big dicks. It's dirty. There's passion..."

Yes, passion's what we're after, and not from Liz Taylor. And we're looking, searching, hoping for some imagination. From the literally thousands of scenes that have been shot over the years, we have picked a few that practically melted our television sets, from artists of sex. We call them artists because it is the artist's gift to see something familiar anew and to make it beautiful, making it the creme de la creme of erotica.

Best Gay Erotic Videos of the Year

(In Alphabetical Order)

"A Summer of Sex" and "The Travelling Journeyman"

It was a bumper crop of riches for the fans of Jean-Daniel Cadinot. First, his story of two French students who spend their summer vacation in Germany matches his previous outings for script, cinematography and witty satire, plus offers the challenge of German hosts who have to be drunk or forced into gay sex. It's all very easy back in France, however, in the splendid "Travelling Journeyman," a humdinger about a farmhand who gets involved with the boss's son. "Add a jealous brother and a constantly horny staff of stable boys and you have the ingredients for as much hot action as one could stand in one sitting," raved Sid Mitchell. One sitting my ass, this one's good for a week's worth of viewing before bedtime. The score is by Myriam Zadeck, winner of the AVN award for best original music in a gay video and he shows the rest just how much the right music can add to the erotic pleasure.

"Campus Glory Holes"

Director Cyrus Dozier and cinematographer Jack Marshall teamed to make the best tearoom action film since Steve Scott's 1981 "Dangerous." Although they didn't delve into the why of public sex, the men presented the seemingly limitless variations available with the emphasis on collegiate types. The video was supposedly filmed "on location at the men's room of a major university" and it has the kind of classy look that can only come when the people who made it actually cared about what they were doing. They took the time to hire a good cast and put them through their paces. Outstanding are Chris McKenzie and Rocky Knight as a couple of jocks and Bobby Balboa as a chickenish-type whose father teaches at the school and who is looking to expand his sex education. The secret to this venture's success is the structure; it permits sequences to overlap as the camera moves from one part of the tearoom to the other, involving the viewer as few films do these days. This has its drawbacks: a dull stretch at the beginning and camerawork that makes the viewer become disoriented, not knowing what group of men he is watching at any given point, which often happens when trying to film an orgy sequence, but from an artistic standpoint, this is a small price to pay for a satisfying experience for those who get off on this type of sex.

"The Devil and Danny Webster"/"Headbangers"

Hot off "The Devil and Danny Webster," Billy Houston cemented his postition as the best newcomer of the year with "Headbangers," two Richard Lawrence videos from Avalon. If your taste runs to young and hung, these two are nearly perfect diversions. About "Headbangers," David Kinnick said: "Houston, a truly fine little actor, plays Chris, the new boy in town with hopes of becoming a guitar player in a band. He worships a very silly rock idol type named Nikki Steele, played by very silly rock idol type Tommy Wilde, who opens the show with an attempt at a rock video. The camera discovers him in a cage wearing tight lycra pantaloons and lip-synching badly to an original song." Several scenes intrude before Billy gets Tommy and at the end there's even a mock wedding. "Overall," Kinnick said, "it's a fun and often hot trip to a world that is a hairdresser's nightmare but probably the best youth-oriented video of the year." Together, "The Devil and Danny Webster," in which Houston realizes he's "gorgeous," and this one make for many a memorable evening for lovers of youth.

"Jackaroos"

It seems that no annual list of the best these days is complete without an entry from Kristen Bjorn. His second trip to Australia (the first brought us "A Sailor in Sydney") departs from the urban environs to give us a glorious journey through the Outback. Rocks, pools and secluded ranch houses provide effective backdrops to the carrying on of hunky dudes who seem to be intensely into what they are doing. A loving couple and three trios appear in the four vignettes, the highlight for us size-queens being the foot-long Sean and his two buddies. They even wear rubbers. Kinnick raved: "Impossible thought it may seem, this eighth video by Bjorn in just two short years is his best yet. Nonstop sex." Bjorn went to the beach for the third in his Australian gambits, "Manly Beach," also with sterling results.

"Motor Punks"

Danny Droids directed a cast of young eccentrics from San Francisco in a little change of pace home video. Dave Kinnick: "As free-form orgies go, this video is a low-budget smash. Every member of the cast is exciting, unknown, and subcultural, the kind of alternate-stream performers that gay porno desperately needs. They are young, bespiked, and destined someday far from now to die with their Doc Martens on. The sex is high energy and hot throughout, which makes up for most of the problems." The four-way cum shot halfway through is a sight to behold. While Mickey Skee panned the film he had to admit the shot of two guys butt-fucking in the rafters of a house, shot from below, was fascinating. These days, little moments mean a lot.

"Muscle Ranch"

Mega-masculine men doing things you'd never believe they would do have always turned-on the gay male audience. The more macho the man the greater the turn-on. This Rip Colt production through Buckshot, is almost a two person show with Jake Tanner and Ed Dinakos, with abundant images of he-manly sex. *Manshots* raved: "The give and take is perfectly balanced, each gives as enthusiastically as he takes. Both have seemingly bottomless gullets and considering the equipment each totes, the deep-throating is downright stupefying." But, ultimately, it's a dry hump because the boys never get around to fucking each other. If they had, this one would have been a masterpiece.

"Pay to Play III"

Before retiring, Vivid's Patrick and Dennis team gave us a sequel that's better than both its predecessors put together, the team's best work since 1989's "Davey and the Cruisers," according to some. Sid Mitchell raved: "A witty cohesive script, modelled after detective films of the '40s and a virtually flawless performance, both dramatically and sexually from Scott Hogan...I suggest you watch this three times: first for the sex, second for the dialogue, and third for the two combined." But enough of this film noir black and white technique. As Josh Eliot says, "The audience isn't into gimmicks." Two of this video's most interesting sexual moments are the tail end flip-flop fuck with Hogan and the Jason Ross/Jason Cruise pairing. Unintentional hilarity comes from the numerous dissolves into plants, ala early Higgins. And mention must be made of star Steve Sinclair, returning as the snotty little hustler, failing miserably to ignite any sexual heat whatsoever, making you think he must be sleeping with the directors in order to keep appearing in these segments.

"Prince Charming"

Amid all the misfires during the year, Jim Steel and his crew at Vivid managed to pull out a winner with this spoof of every gay man's dream: To meet his knight in shining armor and live happily ever after. Sid Mitchell comments: "Brian Yates rips up the screen in a magnificent dual-role performance as the innocent, much-abused Prince Charming and his cynical, wicked twin Prince Blackheart. The final scene, in which Charming meets his true love (newcomer Adam Archer) combines lustful passion with sentimental romance to rank among Steel's most accomplished sexual scenes...the script combines down-and-dirty sex with outrageous satire that includes genuinely funny anachronisms as well as imaginative sexual innuendo."

"Read My Lips"

It seems with some entries, Chi Chi La Rue sets porn back for decades, then he comes up with a gem, showing that if he took the time he could come up with something good. This one for Hard Body Productions with Joe Rock doing the sharp cinematography, "Read My Lips" is arguably the best thing he's done. The hook to hang the sex sequences here is simply a kid dreaming but that's plenty. The voice-over is clever, a dusky voice whispering things like "Yeah, you know you want it" and "Who are you?" But for the anally-fixated, the problem with all-oral films like this is that they seem like so much foreplay, leaving us anxious for more, especially when we've seen beauties like Damien before and know what he can do in that situation. At least we get some great shots of the sweet-lipped exotic Damien kissing. As one of the best kissers (and suckers) in the business, the star makes this one, in this era of romance, downright heartening (if not completely hardening). Mickey Skee concurred: "Wild-haired Damien of the sleek, supple bod is the most exciting." Working on his usual miniscule budget, Chi Chi was desperate for a different look so he stretched one of his nylons over the lens. This gives the whole thing what Dave Kinnick called "Sensual perfection," with "exotic camera lenses and filters, moody lighting, and an incredibly hot dirty talk narration." With this hit, Chi Chi does more for safe sex cocksucking than anybody around.

Best Boxcover

Because most people select what they rent or buy by mail by the boxcover, it is appropriate that quality rewarded. The picks of the year have to be "Read My Lips" and "Scoring," both of which feature the exotic Damien in exotic poses, one a close-up in keeping with the oral action of the former. We select these not only because they are stunning photographed and presented but also because they do not rip-off the consumer. As Dave Kinnick explains, because a boxcover is shot a couple of weeks before a video is taped, in most cases they tell the consumer almost nothing about the contents. Further, they are often put into print production before the video is edited. Consequently, someone can be listed in the credits and never appear in the finished video.

Kinnick further elucidates: "Most people don't fully understand that in the porn business of the '90s, box covers cost almost as much to make as the videos they enclose. It was discovered several years ago, in what I call the 'In Hand Experiment,' that a crummy $6,000 movie in a pretty $2,000 box sells better than a good $12,000 movie in a $500 box. InHand put out 55 titles between '88 and '90 using this stratagem and it propelled that company into one of the top positions in the gay video industry almost overnight." Now everybody follows their example.

And InHand keeps rolling out the slime. In fact, arguably the worst video of the year, if not of all time, came from their machine. We had thought they had sunk to a new low in rip-offs and spin offs when they released the cock-eyed "Batdude and Throbbin" but with "Butt Boys in Space" they outdid themselves. Kinnick hit the right tone: "Imagine the worst possible future for the human race. Now imagine it with colored lights. We've seen this sort of cheesy rip-off of science fiction ever since some smart guy decided the monolith in 2001 might be good for something other than babysitting chimps. But this is the worst possible kind: $1.99 sets and costumes...dime store lighting and a sorry excuse for a script. Gorgeous cover-boy Brett Winters is really wasted in his one scene here and the rest of the cast, the ones you can make out through the haze, are forgettable. The only glimmer of fun is huge-dicked Michael Brandon getting banged for the first time on video." In an interesting sidebar, the same director, Hank Warner, was responsible for last year's "The Grip of Passion," which Mark Glascock of *Southern Exposure* rated "A" for "Awful," too bad because it featured the last film appearance of cute Billy London, who was murdered two days after the film was wrapped. And this is the same Hank Warner who released "Sunday Brunch" through VCA/ HIS also featuring Brett, and by the time the final credits roll, his name has been changed to William Ricche. Whatever his name is, he's guilty of the two worst videos of the year and three of the worst of all time.

The All-Time Best of the Best in Gay Erotica

Best Topping

Pick: Surely the most controversial category but we have to go with Tom Steele with Doug Niles in "Undercover." We may never see the likes of this again, a sex scene that holds up after many repeated viewings. Take one massively hung stud and one alleged straight man who loves to get fucked and you end up with two orgasms from each of them and a sequence that begs to be savored over and over again. About this sequence, and this extraordinary video, critic Sid Mitchell wrote: "Erotic tension is established in the first scene, maintained throughout, and finally released in the superbly photographed encounter between stars Tom Steele and Doug Niles. If I were abandoned with my VCR on some proverbial urban island and could have only one gay video with me, this would be it."

Videographer Josh Eliot recalls: "It's the best movie that's ever been done. Everything about it works, except for the opening dialogue. The whole crew up in San Francisco was really into that film. I can't explain it, but it was such a positive atmosphere. I think it's one of the hottest films ever made, and as far as videography, I think that's the film I really did my best on. Doug Niles has a natural screen presence...Both models really did get into each other. When you're filming a romantic scene as opposed to more of a lust scene, your style is a lot different. You work a lot more with the kissing, the rubbing, the massage."

And, after a couple of mis-fires, including "Powerline" and "Soldiers," Steele proved his mettle, not only here but the superb topping of Beau Beaumont in "Pledgemasters" and Tim Lowe in "Offering," while Tim's screwing a harlot.

Historical Pick: Kip Noll and Jon King in "Kip Noll, Superstar." This was an unexpected bonus tacked on to the end of the first, and still the best, compilation of scenes featuring an erotic performer's body of work. While the sequences are, naturally, all from Kip's appearances for William Higgins, each is as exceptional as the star they feature, but the real kick is Kip and Jon going at each other in the all-new final scene. Although the sexual tension is reduced greatly by unusually poor camerawork for a Higgins production (the cinematographer must have been jacking off a lot) and frequently inadequate lighting, the thrill these two get out of each other as they get it on is infectious, a joy to behold, to be treasured forever.

Runners-up: Kip Noll and the versatile Derrick Stanton in Higgins' classic "Westside Boys;" another sterling demonstration that when two sex machines are turned on, for whatever reason, the results can be magical. Daddy-master Chad Douglas has given us many great scenes of heroic topping. His best include "Below the Belt," "Too Big for His Britches" and, perhaps the very best, "Spring Break's" sequence where the blond twinkie is impaled on the mighty prong, swinging in the air. Also a must is Matt Powers' topping of Vic Summers in "The Main Attraction."

Best Bottoming

Pick: Tim Lowe in "Down Under." We pick this only because we get hetero-humper Tim losing his cherry and liking it so much he just has to do it twice more in the same video. He cums while he's getting it in each sequence and his enjoyment of the whole messy business is infectious.

Runners-up: Hall of Fame Bottoms Jon King and Joey Stefano are incredible in whatever they do but seeing Jon take on both Lee Ryder and Rick Donovan in "The Biggest One I Ever Saw" and Joey with Matt Gunther and Jeff Stryker in "On the Rocks" are scenes not to be missed.

Very Special Mention: Studly Sgt. (and "Safe Sex" spokesman) Glenn Swann bottoming for hugely hung Scott O'Hara in "Private Files."

Best Interracial Sequence

Pick: It would be hard to imagine a more explosive wish-fulfilling interracial segment than the one that caps "One Size Fits All." Director Mark Reynolds wisely chose hunky superstud Lionel Washington to give sensational golden boy Brian Hawks the drilling of his life.

Historic Runner-up: The fantasy a golden boy might have about being had by a huge black stud was superbly captured by director Wakefield Poole in his 1972 classic, "Boys in the Sand." Poole filmed the scene as if blond Casey Donovan, at the top of his game, might just be dreaming the whole thing, which adds to the overall excitement of it.

Second Historic Runner-up: "Ebony Love" (1983) is comprised of four short films directed by Matt Sterling and John Travis during their days at Brentwood and it includes another black telephone repairman (why don't I ever get my phone fixed by anybody like this?) who plugs into a small, white and willing electrician.

Special Mention: We cannot leave the interracial category without mentioning what is arguably the greatest "oreo" sandwich of all time, in Falcon's magnificent 1982 release, "Style," featuring blond gods Tim Kramer and Leo Ford dallying with cute Art Williams, as perfect a specimen of sleek black manhood as you might ever hope to find. (Besides being the star of many black films, Art is also prominent in "Jacks Are Wild" and "J. Brian's Flashbacks.") Sparks fly in this scene.

Best Street Pick-Up

Pick: Everyone dreams of seeing someone on the street and having it develop, within moments, into a magnificent sexual encounter and that's what happens in the opening sequence of an otherwise dismal 1981 film from the Mitchell Brothers, "Cruisin' the Castro." The anonymous dark haired hunk who plays the active role has one of the most beautiful cocks ever preserved on film.

Best Sex in Public Places

Pick: Few films will ever rival "Dangerous" when it comes to this genre, one of director Steve Scott's best efforts. This 1982 release, now distributed by Bijou Video in Chicago, is as provocative an endorsement of casual, anonymous sex as you'll ever hope to see. Superstars Al Parker and Chris Burns appear.

Best Student/Teacher Sex

Pick: "Classmates," made in 1987 by Toby Ross. The scene where the teacher seduces the student, or vice versa, has been a staple of gay erotica since the beginning. It usually comes off as forced, without any tension. Toby Ross solved the problems inherent in this set-up with the first sex episode in "Classmates," practically a movie in itself. Star David Ashfield spends his time in the classroom fantasizing about his youngish, bespectacled art teacher rather than concentrating on his work. The fantasy includes David tempting the teacher with a huge lollipop and a few peeks at the huge candy stick between his legs. The teacher makes David come to his place to study and improve his marks, which leads to David going to bed and asleep, only to be joined by the teacher, who lies next to him, fantasizing about going down on the star. The tenderness expressed as the teacher finally gets the courage to seduce his student is rare in an erotic film. After jacking David off, the teacher rolls over and fantasizes being on his knees, getting fucked by the star doggie-style. After David comes all over his back, the teacher jacks himself to orgasm. Although I would have preferred a more sustained fuck, showing penetration, the scene is beautifully realized.

Runners-up: When Nova closed its doors, its library was sold to L.A. Video, thus preserving many schoolroom fantasies, especially "Something Wild," in which gorgeous Gavin Burke (also known as Rob Montessa) is shown getting fucked by a black professor between the stacks in the school library, after which the star performs auto-fellatio. Another Nova entry in this genre is "Kept After School," in which a macho teacher falls asleep and gets splayed across his desk, then gang-banged by six attractive young students. In "Lockerroom Fever," Tige McMasters is caught by his coach masturbating while holding the coach's jockstrap to his nose. The coach, played by Mitch Taylor, takes Tige over his knee and spanks him, then fucks him. The action continues for the next episode, at the coach's house, where uncut stud Giorgio Canali joins them for a rousing daisy-chain fuck.

Best Dirty Talk
Pick: It'd be hard to select a fouler mouth than that of Jon Vincent, billed in "Heavenly" as "Dave Phillips." He uses the f-word 147 times in the outine In-Hand ski adventure also featuring hot bottom Dany Brown.

Best "Parody of a Hit"
Pick: "Sticky Business." Michael Gere was perfect as the lead in this spin-off of the Tom Cruise blockbuster, "Risky Business." As

lensed by pro photographer Derek Powers, the star's charisma and sexuality pervade the film.

Best Glory Hole Sequence

Pick: Michael Christopher and Jeff Stevens in Steve Scott's masterful light-hearted 1983 hit "Doing It." Anytime you can get stud Michael's perfect piece through a glory hole, you've got something special and the way this one is accomplished makes it a tremendous turn-on. Of all the videos Michael did, this one showcases him best, playing a sexually active older brother. We should all have been so lucky to have had an older brother like him!

Runners-up: The Christy Twins and Jack Wrangler in "Heavy Equipment." The Christies were fresh and fun when this was done and they enjoy Jack's beautiful dick immensely. In "The Bigger the Better," what golden boy Brian Hawks does to four guys in a bathroom includes some hot glory-hole action. And in Higgins' hugely popular 1985 release, "The Young & The Hung," gorgeous Chris Lance swaps blow-jobs with Brian Estevez (here billed as Mike Raymond) through a hole and you'll have to hit the pause button a lot to savor it all.

Also of interest is "Campus Glory Holes," with Chris Mckenzie and a delicious orgy finale.

Best "Sibling" Coupling

Pick: J. W. King and Jon King in William Higgins' 1980 release "Brothers Should Do It!" Many supposed "brothers" are brought together by erotica producers but this one is the most believable of all time and the guys burn up the screen in the finale of this strung-together collection of duos, the rest of which is poorly produced and forgettable. Bill has said he just let the camera run as J. W., by then a durable topman, and Jon enjoyed each other. As Bill said later, "It was magic time."

Best Menage a' Trois

Pick: Streetwise Kip Noll, cutie Scott Noll, and long-donged Steve York in the 1980 release "Cuming of Age." Take the hottest erotic film star of the decade and put him with the size queen's new darling and a fresh-faced little kid and watch what happens!

Simply turn off the ridiculous audio track added later and lie back and enjoy it! When Steve shoves that long hose into little Scott's adorable ass, you can almost feel the delirium that tingles through their lean bodies. As John Rowberry so aptly put it, "Can three guys having sex for an hour keep your attention? Yes, when it's these three guys."

Runners-Up: The supercharged Jon King/Derrick Stanton sequence in Higgins' 1982 release, "Members Only," features one of the best double entries ever captured on film. And don't miss the three-ways in Falcon's "Style," one featuring Leo Ford and Tim Kramer, discussed above, the other featuring Todd Baron and Ron Pearson. They are nothing short of incredible.

Best Orgy

Pick: William Higgins' 1983 classic "Class Reunion." This one rises above all the others because it was conceived as an orgy and overcomes many of the problems inherent in filming a mass fuck-and-suck. When transferred to film, what may have been a gas in person appears cluttered, awkward and ultimately, an uninvolving let-down erotically. This one fails to concentrate on any one particular piece of action for a suitable length of time but the sexual tension that is built up over the course of the film makes it a turn-on. Higgins wisely filled the screen with all of the boys he could find who had been associated with his studio over the years, which included such durables as Leo Ford and Michael Christopher, and he used a Busby Berkeley ("Girl Crazy") approach to some of the scenes, choreographing them to dazzling effect. The daisy-chain is especially memorable. It'll make you wish you'd been there!

Runners-up: The climactic orgy scene in "Boys of Company F," scores, even though the laconic Rick Donovan got lost in the shuffle. A barracks is an ideal setting for an orgy and each of the participants is beautifully put together. 1990's "Lunch Hour," from Josh Eliot and starring Matt Powers, keeps things humming with excellent cross-cutting that keeps your interest. And speaking of daisy-chains, check out the superb one in "Sticky Business," superbly choreographed by cinematographer Derek Powers.

"Oh, God!" cried "Lunch Hour" cinematographer Josh Eliot when asked how he filmed the orgy for this clever, continually absorbing flight of fancy about a gang of studly blue collars who take over their machine shop and force their bosses into submission and sex becomes punishment in the hands of these studs. "Well, my stomach's tied in knots. What I've found to be the easiest way is to split up the action into several groups, get all your master shots first when everybody's in the room - you have eight to ten people and everyone's going to be antsy. For 'Lunch Hour,' I split them up into three groups on top of the machinery, three guys all the way to the left, two guys in the middle, and three guys on the right. Capture them all in the master shot, then move in on one group, and let the other two groups rest. Cover the one group completely up through the oral, close-ups, underneath, then move on to the next group, and the third. Then repeat everything with the anal. All the guys were at the factory the same day, it was a one-day shoot, eighteen hours straight!" Josh followed a similar technique in "Powertool 2," with great results, and Falcon did likewise in "The Abduction."

Best Prison-set Video

Pick: "Lewd Conduct" by recently Federally-indicted director Jim West, who did the deed for Vivid release starring Ted Cox, Eric Ryan, and Sean Fox. Ted plays the obligatory new inmate and David Kinnick wrote, "he largely makes up for the lack of 'prettiness' in the cast by being three times more lovely than anyone deserves. 'Lewd Conduct' will no doubt stand as the definitive gay prison video."

Best Debut

Pick: It came as a total surprise. There, stuck in the middle of Higgins' finest but very predictable travelogue, "Sailor in the Wild," is veteran blond bottom Leo Ford hangin' out at the pool, soon to be joined by a tall, dark-haired stranger with a thick neck...and perhaps the longest cock in gay films at that time. You grabbed the box to see who this was: Rick Donovan! Another star was born! Leo's enjoyment of Rick's meat, beautifully photographed, is a joy. Donovan had performed for Dirk Yates in Seabag's "Military Maneuvers" but Higgins' video was released first (in 1983) and made the top an instant star.

Runner-up: A similar situation developed with Tim Lowe. Seabag honcho Dirk Yates discovered him but Catalina was the first to unleash his power upon the masses. The video was John Travis'

"Powerline" and from the moment the kid comes through the door you know a star has been born. Unfortunately, Travis failed to take advantage of the Lowe magic and it wasn't until Higgins got him to Sydney, Australia, for "Down Under" do we see Lowe get laid not by one but by *two* big-dicked Aussies.

Best Shower Sequence

Pick: For sheer realism, the sequence in the shower in Tom DeSimone's 1979 classic, "The Idol," cannot be topped. As part of a beautifully crafted film about a young man learning to cope with his intense feelings about a track star at school, this scene has incredible erotic tension. A very young Derrick Stanton demonstrates the oral abilities that later served him so well later on in film after film for Higgins.

Best Bisexual Sequence

Pick: Magnificent stud Jeff Stryker dancing around a shower room and then fucking both girl and guy in Travis' immortal 1987 hit "The Switch Is On!" wins this hands down. In the same film, he gets it on with a rich couple in private sauna.

Honorable Mention: Big Tom Steele's smooth fuck of cutie Tim Lowe while Tim fucks a harlot in Paul Norman's "Offering."

Best Gang Rape

Pick: The late Johnny Dawes was young and cute when he got it from a bunch of thugs in the classic "Bad, Bad Boys," a banquet from Tom De Simone which showed another side to the director, taking a social issue of boys driven to the streets to steal explored so famously by Dickens in "Oliver Twist," and neatly turning the tables on the Fagin/stud who tries to manipulate his young charges.

Runner-up: Veteran bottom Dany Brown getting it in "Soldiers," but it's simply too difficult to believe he'd put up much of a fight, and the outstanding sequence in Cadinot's superb "Tough and Tender."

Best Circle Jerk

Pick: (Tie) "The Other Side of Aspen, I and II" are Falcon's spectacularly successful forays into full-length filmmaking. The first edition gave us Casey Donovan, spread-eagled on the coffee table, getting cum splattered all over his face and body by one of the hunkiest gangs ever assembled on film.

Years later, Falcon did it all over again, with Kurt Marshall the recipient of all the juice.

Runners-up: J. Brian's classic "Seven in a Barn" boasts a group of cute boys jacking off and, eventually, getting it on with each other. Brian Hawks' marvelous body and cock are the centerpiece of another highly successful circle jerk in "Brian's Boys," where the fun grows out of the action. And we cannot forget another of Falcon's magnificent full-length features: "Spokes." Seldom has such a heavenly gang of hunky bodies been gathered to enjoy each other. It's more than a circle jerk, of course, but it's not really an orgy either...it's basically a one helluva of a good time.

The Best Gay Videos of All Time

When selecting "The Best" of anything, it's always helpful to establish the criteria for choosing the hottest of the hot. In the case of naming the very best of so many good ones, we based our selections on a consensus of opinion, including reviews from magazine critics we respect, and the general public. The films are judged on over-all filmmaking excellence and how the eroticism was enhanced by the general context of the film. Truly, each of these is a classic in its own right, setting standards by which all others are judged, and deserves to be a part of everyone's permanent collection of gay erotica.

We divide this listing into two sections: the historical significant films and those of more recent vintage that have proven popular with critics and fans alike.

Historically Significant Gay Erotica

"The Back Row" (1973)

Casey Donovan was coming off the hit "Boys in the Sand" and super-hot when he made this one and it was darling little George Payne's debut. They never looked better and are superb together; the hanky-panky in the theatre's john crackles with the genuine heat of spontaneity. By today's standards, you're taken aback that it's being told completely without dialogue, then you realize it doesn't need any, the action speaks volumes.

"Bijou" (1972)

Talk about sexual tension! First we get superhung Bill Harrison in the shower and then we follow him to the movies. A dazzling cinematic experience not to be missed.

"Boys in the Sand" (1972)

Wakefield Poole set out to film something that would not bore gay audiences and he created a classic and made a star of Calvin Culver (aka Casey Donovan.) Only four sequences, but they are choice.

"Brian's Boys" (1983) and "Something Wild" (1984)

Robert Walters created two masterpieces. The former starred Brian Hawks with a bunch of fresh faces and although it is disjointed at the end, for chicken-hawks, it's continually fascinating. The latter stars perhaps the most beautiful young man ever to do an erotic video, Gavin Burke (aka Rob Montessa) as well as the unbelievable Bobby Madison (here billed as Brian Michaels), in a video that shows how loops can be strung together for maximum effect. It uses the shopworn theme about two college kids on a hiking trip sharing tales around a campfire and does it with more imagination and sexual heat than almost any video since.

"Heatstroke" (1982) (and the Joe Gage Trilogy)

Joe Gage's body of work must be considered a piece: the trilogy and "Heatstroke" for good measure. If you like men mature and raunchy action, the Gage library, including the trilogy ("Kansas City Trucking Co.," "El Paso Wrecking Co.," and "L. A. Tool & Die") is as close to perfection as we are likely to see in gay erotic cinema. As with most sequels, "Kansas City Trucking Co." (1976) is the still best, but Richard Locke's performance in all shows, in the words of Sid Mitchell: "... his flair for comedy and sexual stamina that makes him one of the best actors in the history of gay films." Richard also appears in "Heatstroke," about the men at a rodeo in Montana, of which, as John Rowberry said, "After a decade, it is still scorching."

"I Do!" (1984)

Steve Scott created several great videos and this is one of them, proving you can be witty and sexy at the same time. "A tight story, perfectly told," raved John Rowberry about the tale of a kid who finally gets to his brother before he gets married.

"The Idol" (1979)

Tom DeSimone (Lancer Brooks) created a classic with this story of a young man who falls hard for a track star and he was able to get perfect performances from every one of his actors, most of all by handsome Kevin Redding in his one and only screen appearance. Sid Mitchell: "One of the few X rated films to achieve true pathos."

"Kip Noll Superstar" (1981)

The best compilation of a porn star's work ever produced, blessed with the addition of a sizzling scene with Jon King as the final kick. Higgins has said that Kip needed some money and agreed to do this. The director scrambled to write a script and get the deed done before the star changed his mind, which he did frequently.

"Private Collection" (1983)

Six scenes by three superb directors of early erotica make this a short course in contemporary gayporn.

"Style" (1982)

Of all the Falcon "loop groups," this one is the most stylishly put together. It was cast with an eye for what types work together and each scene is a sizzler.

"Wanted" (1980)

Steve Scott's exciting, well-done reworking of "The Defiant Ones" made Al Parker a star and set the standard for how to use a plot to hold together the sex sequences. Jack Wrangler, playing a sadistic guard, was never better.

The Top Gay Erotic Films of All-Time

"All of Me" (1983)

Some reviewers prefer "Dream Boys," released a little earlier the same year, to this because it is a three episode movie, affording a sample of Jean-Daniel Cadinot's marvelous ability to sustain a certain mood, but this beautifully rendered film was my first Cadinot experience and, as a chickenhawk, I was jolted beyond belief, never to forget it. And the director's brilliant success with American audiences like me over the past few years demonstrates that his attitude is one that should prevail more often among men who make movies for gay consumption. Rather than turning out mindless bilge to turn a buck, why not make something you would enjoy seeing yourself? they should ask themselves.

"I never make a film only to please the public," Jean-Daniel said.

"I work for myself; if others happen to enjoy my work, fine. I always have several themes in mind, and when I find the actors who can help me realize those themes, men I myself am attracted to, then I make a film."

"All of Me" stars Pierre Buisson as a youngster who comes Cadinot's studio to interview for a modeling job:

"How old are you?"

"Eighteen."

"Have you ever modeled before?"

"No."

"You seem to be very proud of your cock. Do you like to pose?"

"Yes, it really turns me on." (The boy's tongue and wet lips promise everything and his dark eyes hide nothing. He oozes sex.)

"So I see...that's really a big one. Have you been out long?"

"Not very."

Reel life or real life that begins like that has to become an all-time classic.

"Below the Belt" (1985)

Philip St. John left the business after this, his second feature, and it's a shame. "So effective is the karate aura that it nearly suffices in the absence of any plot to give the work its shape and heat," *Manshots* wrote. It's simply a series of loops, but what a series! The double buttfuck of Michael Cummings by David Ashfield and Scott O'Hara must be seen to be believed and daddy-master Douglas is at his peak in this one, which is incredible indeed.

"Behind Closed Doors" (1989)

Falcon at its best, setting up the fantasy of peeking through keyholes. Studly Tom Steele and Mike Ramsey (returning to gay videos) take turns sharing Mike Gregory for a wow finale.

"Big Guns/Hot Rods" (1987)

Supposedly these two videos, "Hot Rods" being the sequel to "Big Guns," are the last that William Higgins actively participated in before being banished to a life of globe-trotting and they are the epitome of sex in military drag. The director gave each of his off-duty officers a rationale from wandering from the straight-and-narrow and the end result is thrilling indeed, especially the sequence with Kevin Williams, who is always a joy, as is Kevin Wiles, who also bottoms for the studs in this one. To quote *Manshots*: "Three hours of eroticism at its most masterful."

"The Bigger the Better" (1984)
This is the production that made Matt Sterling's reputation because the sex simply never quits. The stars include Rick Donovan, Mike Ramsey and Buster.

"The Biggest One I Ever Saw" (1984)
The directorial debut of Bill Harrison (maginificently long-pronged star of the classic "Bijou") under the name of Ronnie Shark proves a star can have other talents and the result is one of the best military vehicles ever. The 3-way with Lee Ryder, Rick Donovan and Jon King is worth its weight in gold.

"Carnival in Venice" (1987)
Cadinot's sumptuously filmed story of Julien, visiting the city with his parents, and his obsession with a handsome Venetian ladies' man named, naturally, Romeo. A delicious orgy sequence features a few women in the mix. Cadinot's signature work, not the hottest, but plenty hot enough.

"Fratrimony" (1989)
Magazine mogul/video producer Jerry Douglas' masterpiece; the only gay video to feature just two people, but what two people: Tim Lowe and Butch Taylor, getting it on as brothers. Tim never needs to do another thing; his superb performance assures his place in gay film history.

"Heat in the Night" (1989)
Matt Sterling's first video in two years (after "Stryker Force") was a let-down to some (David Kinnick thought it was all much too calculated for its own good) we must agree with John Rowberry who said it had "lots of hot sex beautifully photographed and edited." What John liked and we what liked was the amazing scenes Sterling was able to capture, including the unbelievable sight of Tom Steele deepthroating Dick Masters!

"Inch by Inch" (1985)
Beautiful men, fine photography, superb production values. These are the hallmarks of a Matt Sterling production and never was it more in evidence than here. "Pure erotic gold," Sid Mitchell wrote.

"Island Fever" (1989)
Kristen Bjorn's camera makes love to ten breathingly handsome, built, hung, and generally uncut beauties who cum without even touching themselves. As critic Mark Glascock put it, "There's enough good stuff here to almost require a yardstick to do it justice." Ninety minutes of pure pleasure. You can tell he cares about his work.

"Lifeguard On Duty" (1990)
Little sex bomb Ted Cox gets fucked by megastud Matt Powers. What could be finer?

"Like a Horse" (1984)
Matt Sterling, working direct-to-video, is a superb photographer and, of all his incredibly beautiful films, this and "The Bigger The Better" are the definitive ones. Reviewer John Sarlopoulos said, "'Like a Horse' will show you what gay sex is all about." Indeed, in "Horse," Brian Hawks and Mike Ramsey make a stunning team and the four-way with Steve Henson that climaxes the film is eye-popping. Brian repeated in "Bigger" by taking on four guys in a school bathroom, to maximum effect.

"Main Attraction" (1987)
Unquestionably Scott Masters' masterpiece, with the remarkable scenes on a bus with hunky blond stud Keith Panther at his best and mud wrestling with Peter Ashley and Tim Lowe, with Tim playing bottom, plus the climactic romantically dreamy fuck of Vic Summers by uncut Matt Powers, this one has everything.

"Matter of Size" (1984)
Bill Henson is just one of a dozen incredibly beautiful men in Matt Sterling's voluptuous first outing on his own after leaving Falcon

Studios.
"More Than a Man" (1990)
The self-proclaimed "sex maniac" Joey Stefano glows in Jerry Douglas' signature work about a confused Catholic boy. The barroom fuck is worth the price of a rental. *Gay People's Chronicle* reviewer Rex Rod: "You know this video is going to be different when it opens with Joey Stefano on his knees, in front of an altar, that is, with a rosary in hand." And different it is, perhaps the best gay video of the '90s so far, it has a dynamite barroom menage a' trois, Joey getting it from Chris McKenzie and Lon Flexx, as the lucky patrons look on. The only misfire is the Rick Donovan/Stefano pairing. Rick just couldn't get the big one hard for the infamous bottom.

"Night Flight" (1985)
When Falcon tackles a sustained narrative, they do a sensational job. This affords many pleasures and one of the biggest ones is incredible black stud O. G. Johnson. Plus the beautiful blond, the late Kurt Marshall at his prettiest.

"Pleasure Beach" (1983)
The late director Arthur Bressan's legacy, this is, to quote John Rowberry, "Gay porn at its finest." Michael Christopher and Johnny Dawes have a summer of love and sweep us along with them.

"Pledgemasters" (1989)
Falcon's neat little package of relentless sex at a frat house, featuring a sterling cast including Tom Steele, Steve Hammond and Beau Beaumont (here billed as Ryan Edwards).

"Powertool" (1986)
Jeff Stryker at his gay best, which is very nice indeed. John Travis' masterpiece about men behind bars won the AVN award for Best Picture.

"Sailor in the Wild" (1983)
Even though the films of William Higgins are short on plot and characterization, they have become best sellers and continue to sell strongly because of the master's knack for discovering succulent

young men, his unfailing ability to create situations which are conducive to sizzling carnality and his skill as a cinematographer to capture the experience onto celluloid.

Beginning with "The Boys of Venice" in 1978, Higgins followed an interesting formula, holding the action together with a theme, more often than not geographical. His "Rear Deliveries" set in motion an alternate formula, utilizing warehouses or delivery boys as the theme. The Higgins company, now called Catalina Productions, was the first to jump on the bi-sexual bandwagon and has also discovered the marketability of the "striptease" male videos, which can be marketed to women as well as men. Clearly, under Higgins, there was no studio that had the marketing savvy of Catalina.

What was so surprising about Higgins, and the organization he founded, that despite his reputation for being a controversial figure in the industry, he earned high marks from the models, that they can always get a fair shake from him, that he's either given them what they asked for or at least what they earned, and that he never promised anything he didn't deliver. Bobby Madison, for instance, recalls: "He's been a tremendous help to me in many, many areas. He's been more than generous, more than understanding, more than fair. I feel he's genuinely concerned about my well-being. He's a man of many interests and he doesn't have time for anyone who is not honest and straightforward. Unlike a lot of the people in this business, he doesn't talk down to you. I don't expect to be categorized and treated like rough trade simply because the last person someone worked with was. If you're fair with him, Mr. Higgins' interest goes far beyond when the camera stops rolling. He's helped me out of some very tight situations."

While some critics feel "Pacific Coast Highway" as Higgins' signature work, we feel of all of his travelogues, "Sailor" is truly one of the all-time best because not only is it probably his most popular but also because its theme is more cohesive, the performance of Brian Thompson in the lead and the undeniable fact that every scene is a winner, including the debut of Rick Donovan.

"Screenplay" (1984)

Steve Scott took his cast and crew to the Lost World Resort in Palm Springs and created a unique, marvelously-crafted piece of cinema magic that rivals much more expensive theatricals for production values, including it's classy titles (The Font Shop) and an original theme song, "Lookin'," sung by Robert Kimbrough. Wildly popular when it was first released, this video endures in rental stores. Its best scene is an unforgettable bang of the best bottom in the business, Jon King, by one of the best tops in the business, Lee Ryder. Fred Bisonnes, writing in *Advocate Men*,: "Both Ryder and King unload extravagantly, Jon bucking and growling/howling all the way!" Bisonnes feels Steve was "one of the few directors of real merit in gay porn." *Stallion Magazine* called him "the class act of gay porn."

Besides "Screen Play," Scott directed the early Al Parker hits, "Inches" and "Wanted," and the best sellers "Dangerous" and "Games." His three films for TCS Studio, "I Do," "Doing It" and "Gold Rush Boys," are neat little features with attractive young casts that never fail to please viewers.

"Sex Bazaar" (1982)/"Sex Oasis" (1989)

"Sex Bazaar," honored as the Best Foreign Film in 1984, the year it was released here, by the now defunct Gay Producers Association, is an amusing little movie identified with Cadinot. He didn't direct, only produced, but it employs the exotic locales and brilliant camera work that is his specialty. The story, about a young French tourist goes to Casablanca and gets fucked a dozen times in the course of a single day, will have special appeal for those into uncut males and multi-racial types, with the emphasis on black studs.

Cadinot himself was later to tackle a similar idea in "Sex Oasis," and, staging it with the epic scale of "Carnival in Venice," created a masterpiece containing, as John Rowberry so aptly put it, "some of the best butt-fucking you've ever seen." It's the story of a young German who gets stranded in North Africa and what transpires when his brother comes to save him. This one has subtitles but doesn't need them; it has plenty of the universal language, which transcends any need for translation.

"Sizing Up" (1984)

Matt Sterling pulled out all the stops in this gritty, often harsh games-inspired thriller.

"Skin Deep" (1983)

"Richly dramatic, abashedly romantic, relentlessly arousing. Thoughtful script, believable acting and sexual performances, plentiful production values, vivid camera work, memorable visual images, and superlative sensual score." That's the way one reviewer described this uniting of Michael Christopher and Johnny Dawes, hot off of "Pleasure Beach," this time for Tom DeSimone of "The Idol."

"Too Big for His Britches" (1988)

Bill Harrison (long-dicked star of the Golden Age of Porn winner "Bijou") followed up his blockbuster the success, "The Biggest One I Ever Saw," with this deft look at all the things that can happen on one's way to a job interview. Among the delights: The big Chad Johnson, Chad Douglas getting deep-throated by Cory Monroe and the beautiful Leigh Erickson playing a horny motorcycle cop! Wow!

"Tough and Tender" (1984)

A youngster is sent to a reform school in the French countryside in this stunning film from Cadinot. After a brutal anal inspection by the sinister medical staff he is put in a large dormitory and, within a few moments after lights out, he is brutally raped by the rest of the boys. This is no half-hearted attempt of a rape scene. This is Cadinot at his best: it is downright nasty. There is terror in the boy's face as his head is pushed through the bars at the head of the bed and the rest of the guys line up to take a crack at his ass or mouth or sometimes both. The frightening scenario deals with the pecking order of the boys' sordid lives in a society within a society, the strong against the weak, the older boys against the younger, and captured in perfect detail in this powerful but raunchy masterpiece. Cadinot has been questioned about the age of the actors. "Some people find it hard to believe that the youngest-looking actor in 'Tough and Tender' is 20 years old," he said. "For an American he may look 15 or 16. An American boy of 18 or 19 looks to European eyes like 22 or 23. Most of my actors, say 70 to 80% are bisexual. I prefer them." They are bisexuals who, from what shows up on the screen, have a proclivity for anal sex.

"Two Handfuls, Part Two" (1989)

John Summers actually improved on the original by John Travis. His careful attention to detail really pays off in every scene. Dave Kinnick: "This one is art-directed up the butt. Sometimes, more is better." John Rowberry: "Slick series of choreographed mating rituals."

"Undercover" (1989)

The best gay porn film of 1989; Sid Mitchell said if he were banished to an island with his VCR, this would be the gay video he'd want to have. Tom Steele tops at his very best, thanks to a turned-on Doug Niles. John Travis directed, cinematography by Josh Eliot.

The Year's Best in Straight Erotica

If you've always wondered what a gaymale video would be like if somebody with a modicum of talent took the time to do it right, and had a better than miniscule budget, examine a couple of these winners made during the year for straight audiences.

You need only watch the opening title sequence and the "orgy on a dance floor" sequence to prove the point as John Leslie, longtime fucker, becomes writer and director on "Curse of the Catwoman." The results are spectacular. Males assembled to do the work here include Tom Byron and T.T. Boy, and boy do they ever. All the guys are hard throughout and the circle jerk is wonderful, with everyone cumming on the barroom floor. The film was shot with a high tech gloss that adds considerably to the heat by cinematogrphaer Jack Remy. Leslie edited. There's even superb original music by Bill Reid. This is what gaymales could have if the studios released just half the annual output.

Other straight videos voted fully erect for the year included: "The Masseuse" from Vivid, "Wild Goose Chase" from Evil Angel and "New Wave Hookers 2" from VCA. The last-named was a highly successful sequel to one of the funniest adult videos this side of "Deep Throat."

The talented Henri Pachard (Radley Metzger) came back to adult video with two excellent productions, "Hothouse Rose Part 1" (featuring Jeanne Fine, straight porn's best actress, and veteran studs Jon Dough, Tom Byron, and T. T. Boy) and "City of Sin" (also featuring Fine), both filmed by Alex DeRenzy.

The straight genre has it's share of stinkers as well. Al Goldstein of *Screw Magazine* put it best when he said that most porn was third rate stuff made by second rate people. Consider, 20 videos are released every week. At that rate, it's hard to have quality, as *Hustler* magazine noted in their wrap-up of the year's worst: "Whew! Who farted? Oh, it's just some poor soul slipping one of the 'Totally Limp' videos into his VCR." The stinkers included "The Monaco Falcon" (VCA), "L. A. Stories" (Vivid), "Pleasure Seekers" (Vidco), "Confessions of a Chauffeur" (Dreamland), "Pro Ball" (Vidco) and "Steamy Windows" (VCA), proving even the best production houses can have their off days.

After having back doors closed for a few years in straight porn, vigorous butt fucking made a tremendous comeback with the success of the various "Buttman" vehicles of John Stagliano, director of the hit "Wild Goose Chase." This guy, who also appears in his own films, has an obsession with anal that never seems to take a vacation, as evidenced by his latest, "Buttman Back in Rio." His "Buttman's Ultimate Workout" was voted best video of the year by FOXE, Fans of X-rated Entertainment, the people's choice of straight porn.

But the award for the most inventive parody of all in a land of parodies has to go to Paul Norman for "Cyrano," a bastardization of the famous love story about the man with the long ugly nose, only in Paul's case the guy's nose is also his cock, or what Hustler magazine called, "a perpetually perky proboscis prodding primed pussies." And they had to admit that the nose-hose did have "an eerie, erotic appeal," making this video a howler and a half, but only "half erect."

The sluttiest slut in porn award must go to "Harley Sluts" star Trixy Tyler, whose favorite sex act is an orgy. "With as many men as I can get," she says. For "Gang-Bang Girl No.1" there were only 19 guys, but every guy penetrated and every guy came in her mouth. This girl loves cum so much she even drank it out of the rubbers. "There was a big difference in the taste, texture, the body temperature, the smell -every single guy was different." Astounding! And about that guy that ate the broccoli for lunch...

And speaking of guts, the award for the most inspired stage name in straight porn must go to a fellow who calls himself "Petey Balls." Now, that takes balls.

The All-Time Best of Straight Erotica

Hollywood's resident critic of straight erotica, Jim Holliday, who swears he's watched thousands of flicks, composed a list of the best, in consensus with several other critics of triple X-rated output. I have culled from this list of forty, ten that I have found to be particularly enjoyable and enhancing to a gay lifestyle. Any of these are especially useful when courting a straight guy who needs some "encouragement."

"The Opening of Misty Beethoven" (1976)

Directed by Radley Metzger, this film represents the pinnacle of style during the "porn chic" '70s and always makes everyone's list as one of the best of all time. It remains a stand-out because of incredible production values (filmed in France) and superb acting. Gayporn star Casey Donovan plays an important role in the film as well as providing the willing ass for the insert footage of the dildo at the finale.

"Insatiable" (1985)

Directed by Godfrey Daniels, this is porn star and Ivory Snow covergirl Marilyn Chambers at her best, coupling with John Holmes and other studs. You can fast-forward through the lesbian sequences to get to the fuck on the pool table featuring David Morris and then the slambang finale on the same table with Holmes and Mike Ranger. Holmes' gigantic meat never got a better showcase than this. Top-notch production values (it was partly filmed in England) and Marilyn warbling "Shame on You" on the soundtrack make this a must for any collection.

When Marilyn was asked what it was like performing with John, she replied, succinctly: "Painful."

"Deep Throat" (1972)

Directed by Gerard Damiano, this is a classic that must be seen to be appreciated. It's probably made more money than any erotic film and justifiably so because it's a hoot from beginning to end (sample: the faggot, played by Damiano himself: "What's a nice joint like you doing in a girl like that?") Fellatio aficionados will delight in Linda Lovelace's attempts to find the longest dick in the world so she can get off.

"The Private Afternoons of Pamela Mann" (1974)

Directed by Radley Metzger, this was the first big budget porn flick and all that dough shows up on the screen, with a glossy Hollywood feel and a delightful comic edge. Two of the hottest gay stars of the day, Eric Edwards and slim, sexy Marc (10 1/2") Stevens, appear here as private eyes and Barbara Bourbon, the star, actually deep throats Marc's incredible meat in a scene that's a treasure.

"Behind the Green Door" (1972)

Directed by the celebrated Mitchell Brothers, Jim and Art, one later to murder the other, this is a landmark film of its day, teaming blond Marilyn Chambers and black stud Johnny Keyes in kinky action.

"The Devil in Miss Jones" (1972)

Another great erotic film directed by Gerard Damiano, this was the first to deal with serious subject matter, the first to have a real actress in the lead (the insatiable Georgina Spelvin) and the first to offer one of everything except gay: there is oral, straight, anal, lesbian, masturbation, 3-way, kink (bananas and a snake) and a sandwich. Besides the gay sex, the only thing they left out was an orgy, which takes six or more. This set the standard and may never be equalled again.

"Inside Jennifer Welles" (1977)

Directed by Howard A. Howard, this was the first of the "profile" films, clips of hot scenes from a star's extensive output and, in this case, nobody deserved it more than luscious Jennifer Welles. The result is 118 minutes of wall-to-wall sex but much of it is lesbian so fast forward to the final scene that makes it a stand-out for gay audiences: Jennifer services nine guys at a party and then finishes off by taking on the four Oriental waiters!

"The Devil in Miss Jones, Part II" (1983)

Directed by Henri Parchard, this sizzler brings Justine Hones (Georgina Spelvin) back to earth for a sequel and instead of the high drama that marked the original, "Part II" shoots low for high camp. Of interest to gay audiences is the appearance of Jack Wrangler, who is so good as the Devil that he holds the whole thing together.

"Taboo" (1980)

Directed by Kirdy Stevens, this landmark film, which has become one of the biggest sellers in history, looks at incest, mother and son variety, and does it with aplomb. The sex includes a twelve-person daisy chain.

"Candy Strippers" (1978)

Directed by Bob Chinn, this film deserves to become a classic. There is an abundance of pretty people and lots of laughs in a hospital setting, all building to a party orgy that is one of the best ever done. Jim Holliday summed it up best when he wrote, "Ask me to recommend a film that celebrates the joys of sex and this is the first one to come to mind."

Runners-up:

"House of Dreams" (1990)

High class kink from Andrew Blake, famous for "Night Trips" and "Night Trips II." As *Playboy* put it: "As adult vids move into the Nineties, Blake's take the cake."

"Score" (1975)

Directed by Radley Metzger, this was a hard-core release now available only as soft that puts the current batch of bisexual thrillers to shame. Filmed on location on an island in the Adriatic Sea off Yugoslavia, we have kink of the highest order, including a beautifully done romance between Casey Donovan and hunky Gerald Grant. We love the line, "It doesn't matter who you love just so long as you love." Amen.

Afterword

"Your Blood on the Floor"

"How many FBI Special Agents does it take to screw in a light bulb?"
"Thirty. One to do the screwing and 29 to see the bulb doesn't make a getaway."

"What's up?"
"What's goin' on?"
"What the hell is happening here?"

The terrible reality is, most Americans don't know; they simply haven't a clue.

As Stephen-Paul Martin said: "When Samuel Beckett began 'Waiting for Godot' with the phrase 'Nothing to be done,' he captured perfectly the absurdity of living in a world in which all actions seemed at least partially misguided.

"Humility is not a very fashionable word these days -conjuring images of lobotomized Fundamentalists banning textbooks and hunting blacks and homos in the name of God-but this word is nonetheless a crucial part of our current situation.

"What is there for a truly intelligent person to do except to admit that he or she doesn't know what's going on?"

As Robert Scheer says: "Consider the anomaly here. The bedrock of freedom is the notion that bad ideas will be defeated not by censorship but by exposure. That's why we let characters such as Andrew Dice Clay rant."

About the carrying-on at the Kitty Kat Lounge in Indiana, Justice Byron White said (in his dissenting opinion): "The performers may not be high art and may not appeal to the Court, but it is hardly an excuse for distorting and ignoring the settled doctrine."

Clyde DeWitt of the Beverly Hills legal firm of Weston and Sarno: "Obviously, a number of Americans profess (as is their constitutional right) to support the proposition that sex should only occur between persons of the opposite sex who are married and only have procreation in mind. Although the number of Americans actually behaving that way is profoundly smaller, the anti-sex movement has managed to infiltrate the highest reaches of our government. It uses Sunday-morning peer pressure to obtain signatures on petititions (such an activity, of course, is protected by the First Amendment) and get all kinds of political attention. The result is that those in power have embraced the anti-sex position.

"The difference between a free society and one which is not is whether government suppresses communication which expresses or encourages points of view which are inconsistent with those of the powers that be; in a free society, communication encouraging all points of view are legal. In a non-free society, they are not."

There are those who would like this to be about as non-free as you can get. In fact, there is what has been called a "conspiracy" to wipe out sex in America. One of the vangards of this movement is the Reverend Donald Wildmon of the American Family Association, numbering 750,000 zealots.

"The reason Rev. Wildmon is in the business of selling fear," Al Goldstein feels, "is that he can make good money at it. Every time he sends out a boycott newsletter, he includes a request for funds. This year, he's spending $1 million pushing his tastes on America, and much more just to keep his ministry afloat. It would be easy to ignore him but people thought if they ignored Hitler he'd go away."

The actor Robert Foxworth: "...the Wildmons of the world -and they proliferate as soon as one demonstrates he can get headlines and effect - must be fought in kind. " He recommended a buycott instead of a boycott. For every item that Wildmon said he didn't want us to buy because they sponsored an unobjectionable TV program, Foxworth said we should buy it. Goldstein agreed; he told all his girlfriends to use Barbosol (one of the banned products) to shave their pussies. Noting that more than a few corporate giants have backed down in the face of pressure, Foxworth goes on to suggest that people write letters of thanks to the banned companies.

Justice White notwithstanding, another group it's hard to ignore is the new Supreme Court. It will probably confront the constitutionality of obscenity forfeiture statutes and other issues sooner rather than later. Where the new justice, Clarence Thomas, stands on porn is a question. Stray pubic hairs on his Coke can notwithstanding, porn, and its assumed link with sexual excess and depravity, loomed large in the hearings on the confirmation of the Judge. "Thomas's supporters seemed to operate under the assumption that they could prove that he is a 'decent man' if they denied loudly and earnestly enough the possibility that the judge is a porn reader," commented *The Advocate's* columnist S. Bryn Austin. Austin also has harsh words for the President: "Bush used the specter of porn to divert attention away from the issue of sexual harassment. Not long after giving a speech on the perils of pornography, Bush dismissed (Anita) Hill's allegations and declared his unwavering confidence in Thomas." Austin found it amazing that several days after the confirmation, Bush's main concern was that his grandchildren had been exposed to "graphic public discussion of sexual matters," further indicating the President's uncanny ability to "perform extravagant feats of misogynist mental gymnastics."

Mental gymnastics were also at work, as usual, in Congress during 1991, where the rightwing leaders Jesse Helms, William Dannemeyer and Mitchell McConnell tried to ramrod the bill S 1521, known as the "Pornography Victims' Compensation Act," down the throats of the American people. On its surface, the bill has the laudable purpose of compensating the victims of sexual assault, but what it really does is to lay the blame on the "producer, commercial distributor, commercial exhibitor or other seller of obscene material..." for damages. It is, in effect, a reincarnation of the "feminist/antipornography bill" which was declared unconstitutional by the Supreme Court. As attorney Burton Joseph commented, "Too often criminals attempt to rationalize their conduct by claiming it was the tight skirt, the movie they saw on television or an explicit photograph that inflamed them."

No psychiatrist, psychologist, researcher or scholar has ever proven that reading a book or seeing a movie has caused a normal person to assault, rape, kill, or murder, as much as Ed Meese and his ilk would have you believe. As Joseph states, "Through the ages, people have used the Bible to justify their behavior: spare the rod, spoil the child.

"By concentrating on a scapegoat the law allows its sponsors to assume they have done something when actually they are neglecting the real causes of societal violence."

Barry Lynn of the ACLU says: "The truth, in fact, is the opposite. It's a complete lie. They've managed to distort all known scientific evidence with the help of the Meese Commission." In fact, Dr. Loretta Haroian of the Institute for Advance Study of Human Sexuality says: "There is no evidence to suggest that. Most people who view adult materials feel they're helped by it. They felt liberated and grown up. This issue is about freedom. Government harassment can increase to the point where we just let our freedom slip away. Nobody stands up and our rights are just eroded."

Dr. Gary Mongiovi agrees: "Sexual expression is perhaps the most fundamental mainfestation of human individuality. Erotic material is subversive in that it celebrates, and appeals to, the most uniquely personal aspects of an individual's emotional life. Thus, to allow freedom of expression and freedom of thought in this realm is to tolerate, and indeed to promote diversity and non-conformist behavior in general."

About Helms and Dannemeyer, the late Joseph Papp commented: "They're both obsessively homophobic. You'll notice that all the restrictions relate to male activities. They are part of a group of men who are scared of sex, or the indication of sex, and here is their opportunity to do something. And most Americans don't approve of what they are doing but this has enabled them to exploit fears that some Americans have about homosexuals."

Leading the assault on individual freedoms is the FBI. Valid evidence of the Government's theory that any visual depiction of sex is per se obscene has surfaced in one of the many search warrants issued in Los Angeles County over the past year, which included raids on leading producers of gaymale porn such as Vivid, Jeff Stryker's studio, and InHand. The team invading these outfits included a number of "Special Agents" for the FBI. These Special Agents are so-called because they have become "experts in their field." Remember, the following quoted portion of the search-warrant affidavit contains no perjury. The cop in question "has participated in hundreds of investigations and arrests for obscenity violations." He "has received formal academic training and on-the-job training in the field of pornography." After that, he was "utilized as an instructor in the field of pornography." To top it off, he has "viewed hundreds of videotapes, films and magazines which have been used in both Federal and State obscenity cases."

One of his cohorts has been "conducting investigations concerning violations of federal laws involving pornography" for over 12 years, "developing unique expertise and knowledge of the hardcore porn industry." If you are to believe the Meese Commission, et al, such exposure would certainly make these guys dangerous criminals.

Speaking of dangerous criminals, Jim West, veteran director of films for many studios and most often lately for Vivid, was arrested in a sting operation and charged with four counts of "conspiracy to distribute obscene material into Mississippi." He faces five years in prison and a $250,000 fine on each charge. The peculiar thing about this case is that West is a filmmaker yet was charged for distribution. He said: "I have no knowledge how Vivid disperses its product. I make the film, turn it over to them, and move on. It is their right to see it in any legal way they see fit." He says he makes about $1,000 from his efforts and gets no royalties or percentages. "Although I'd heard the phrase, 'freedom of speech,' I had no idea how important it is for us to fight to keep it. I didn't know it, but there's a war going on between us and a small group who would obiliterate our freedom of expression." Now he knows.

One encouraging note as far as gaymales are concerned came in the celebrated trial in Las Vegas of Reuben Sturman, reportedly the biggest wholesaler of porn in the world. A jury of Sturman's peers found that the William Higgins classic "Brothers Should Do It!" was not obscene, but they were deadlocked on "Golden Showers," a urination tape, and others featuring what the jury considered bizarre behavior. Post-trial questioning revealed that the jurors thought the government had presented a very weak case.

It seems very weak cases are de rigeur for the government's number one censor, Patrick Trueman (yes, that's his real name), who runs the National Obscenity Enforcement Unit. It seems he has no choice, feeling pressure from his wife, his neighbors, his church and every pornophobe in the universe. One wonders how many more trials with weak government cases will convince Trueman's bosses that he's doing a lousy job and that they should devote more Justice Department funding to other matters.

The truth is that while Trueman and all his Special Agents and the fundamentalists and the President and the Senators and the Supreme Court demand the loss of basic human rights, assets and even personal liberty of those determined to be involved in activities deemed objectionable to them, most Americans just sit by and watch the spectacle unfold.

Yes, it's a great show, as long as it's not *your* blood on the floor.

186

Dedication

To Corey
...thanks for the memories

On December 23, 1991, Corey Haim turned 20, the same age my lover was when I first met him. In fact, they share the same birthday and, of course, the same sun sign. The similarities don't end there: Both are sandy-haired, blue-eyed bundles of joy, later to become objects of torment for those who loved them. While my ex-lover is an artist and teacher and Corey Haim is a movie star, my devotion to each of them has been boundless.

As many of the teenage heartthrobs have, Corey got his start early on in commercials, from which he graduated to ever-larger roles in films, including "Firstborn" (1983), his debut film, "Silver Bullet," with Gary Busey, "Murphy's Romance" with Sally Field, "A Time to Live" with Liza Minnelli, "The Lost Boys," "License to Drive," "Dream A Little Dream," and "Watchers." My personal favorite of all of his films, "Lucas," was made in 1986 when he was 15.

Somewhere along the way, Corey got into Hollywood's fast lane and couldn't get out. Eventually, his mother got him into rehab and he's recovered, resuming his career. The films he has made over the past few months have all gone direct to video, where we can enjoy them the most anyway.

When he isn't working on a film, a typical day for the star starts at 10 a.m. "I don't start breathing until ten! I hate mornings! Then, I take a shower, eat some breakfast, make some plans, or drive around and do something. If there's nothing special planned, I like to go to Big Bear Lake for the day or the weekend." Sounds like fun to me, too, Corey...hint, hint.

And you have to love a kid who tells you, "I like looking for adventure. It's fun. You don't know what you're going to find."

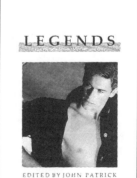

NEW SENSATIONS
from STARbooks Press

Lowe Down: "You're Delivered from the Limits You've Always Felt."

NEW and RECOMMENDED,
from STARbooks Press:
PATRICK, JOHN.
"LOWE DOWN: TIM LOWE."
ISBN 1-877978-22-1. Gay Non-Fiction.
Quality Trade
Paperback; Includes Art Print
Monograph. $9.95 U.S.

In his popular works about gay icons, award-winning author John Patrick screws a microscope to the surface of the flesh in an offhand, understated way, filled with emotion, the effect sneaking up on readers days after they've put the books down, making them want to return to them again.

The latest of Patrick's exposes, "Lowe Down: Tim Lowe," unfolds like a poisonous lotus blossom redolent with luxurious evil. We find that the dilemma of some male sex performers is their own fear of identification with their sense of shame. They play many roles but they must not be gay, for homosexuality is as much a doom as old age. We see erotic star Tim Lowe as a wonderfully engaging character, masculinely seductive, yet boyish, a presence impossible to adequately describe, but Patrick tries: "You find that when you are with him, your mind ticks off the possibilities. Open some doors, he seems to be saying. Walk through any door that suits you. And, as the star of 'Fratrimony' glories in his specialty of making the person he's with feel good, perhaps better than they've felt in a long time, you find you can't describe it, you just enjoy it. You're delivered from the limits you've always felt." In their conversations, the star and the narrator try to be explicit, accurate, to the point. Literature detailing the life of a subculture may have to inform its readers in a self-conscious way and here this informational aspect is stressed, with mechanical objectivity, and the reader revels in a sense of seeing another kind of life through a convenient one-way glass.

Around the intercourse of the collaborators, the author weaves a story of romantic possession, scholarly possession of the past and those possessed by the past, packed with sexual scrimmages. The author uses his beloved New Orleans to good effect. Of all American cities, it is the least Puritan and the most resistant to English priggishness, the perfect setting for the implacable author to dissolve normal life with his erotic dream logic as the book becomes a trip through dazzling fantasies which become more and more unhinged. Sometimes daring, "Lowe Down" is always dutiful, authentic and insightful.

Acknowledgements

The editor thanks our long-time editor J.C., Art & Mike and the many contributors of considerable discernment where things of this nature are concerned without whose invaluable assistance this book would not have been possible.

We also thank Brown Bag Company for use of the photographic image of Billy Houston, appearing in "The Devil and Danny Webster" and "Head Bangers," Avalon releases available from Brown Bag. For a complete catalogue of Brown Bag adult entertainment offerings, write to P. O. Box 1067, Los Angeles CA 90078 or call 800/222-9622. (Offer restricted in some states.)

And we thank the incomparable photographers Bruce Weber, whose latest books "Bear Pond" and "Bruce Weber" are available from STARbooks Press, and Herb Ritts, whose work, "Duo," is also available from STARbooks Press.

For a complete catalogue of STARbooks Press offerings, write: P. O. Box 2737, Sarasota FL 34230-2737.

About the Editor

The author relaxing in Florida with erotic star Tom Steele.

John Patrick is a prolific, prize-winning author of fiction and non-fiction. One of his short stories, "The Well," was honored by PEN American Center as one of the best of 1987, and became the basis for the book "The Bigger They Are," now part of his "Angel: The Complete Quintet," which has become an international best-seller. The author's other acclaimed romans a' clef, "Billy & David: A Deadly Minuet," "Strip: He Danced Alone," and "The Kid," as well as his unique series of erotic books about gay icons, including "The Best of the Superstars," "A Charmed Life: Vince Cobretti," "Lowe Down: Tim Lowe," and "Legends: The World's Sexiest Men," as well as his new non-fiction novel, "What Went Wrong? When Boys Are Bad & Sex Goes Wrong," continue to gain him new fans every day.

A member of the American Booksellers Association, American Civil Liberties Union and the American Booksellers Foundation for Free Expression, the author is the divorced father of two children and now resides on an island in Florida.